The Making
Friends Program

The Making Friends Program

Supporting Acceptance in Your K–2 Classroom

by

Paddy C. Favazza
University of Massachusetts Boston

Michaelene M. Ostrosky
University of Illinois at Urbana-Champaign

and

Chryso Mouzourou
Ohio State University
Columbus

with contributors

Lisa M. van Luling, Psy.D., Lori E. Meyer, Ph.D., SeonYeong Yu, Ph.D.,
Hyejin Park, Ph.D., Emily A. Dorsey, Ph.D.

·P·A·U·L·H·
BROOKES
PUBLISHING Co®

Baltimore • London • Sydney

Paul H. Brookes Publishing Co.
Post Office Box 10624
Baltimore, Maryland 21285-0624

www.brookespublishing.com

Typeset by Scribe Inc., Philadelphia, Pennsylvania.
Manufactured in the United States of America by
Sheridan Books, Chelsea, Michigan.

Cover image is © istockphoto/SerrNovik.
Clip art is © istockphoto.com.

The individuals described in this book are composites of real people whose situations are masked and are
based on the authors' experiences. In all instances, names and identifying details have been changed to
protect confidentiality.

Library of Congress Cataloging-in-Publication Data

The Library of Congress has cataloged the print edition as follows:

Favazza, Paddy C., 1954- author.
  The making friends program : supporting acceptance in your K–2 classroom / Paddy C. Favazza, Ed.D.,
University of Massachusetts, Boston, Michaelene M. Ostrosky, Ph.D., University of Illinois, Champaign,
Chryso Mouzourou, Ph.D., Ohio State University, Columbus.
    pages   cm
  Includes bibliographical references and index.
   ISBN 978-1-59857-921-5 (pbk.)—ISBN 978–1-68125–054–0 (epub)—
ISBN 978-1-68125–049–6 (kindle)—ISBN 978–1-68125-051-9 (pdf e-book)
   1. Inclusive education—United States. 2. Education, Elementary—Curricula. 3. Education, Elementary—Activity programs. I. Ostrosky, Michaelene, author. II. Mouzourou, Chryso, author. III. Title.
  LC1201.F27 2016
   371.9'046—dc23   2015020422

British Library Cataloguing in Publication data are available from the British Library.

2019   2018   2017   2016   2015

10   9   8   7   6   5   4   3   2   1

Contents

About the Forms

Purchasers of this book may download, print, and/or photocopy the blank forms and sample materials for educational use. These materials are included with the print book and are also available at **www.brookespublishing .com/downloads** with (case sensitive) keycode: 2vaPaR5k.

About the Authors

Paddy C. Favazza, Ed.D., Senior Research Fellow and Professor of Early Childhood Special Education, Center for Social Development and Education, University of Massachusetts Boston, 100 Morrissey Boulevard, Boston, Massachusetts 02125

Dr. Paddy C. Favazza's research focus in social inclusion, attitude development, and social and motor development, with interest in curriculum development. Professor Favazza is a former teacher of young children with disabilities and an advocate for the rights and dignity of all children, committed to ensuring that curriculum and strategies used in early childhood have sound theoretical underpinnings, represent evidenced-based practice, engage families, and are culturally responsive.

Michaelene M. Ostrosky, Ph.D., Head and Professor, Department of Special Education, University of Illinois at Urbana-Champaign, 288 Education, 1310 South Sixth Street, Champaign, Illinois 61820

Dr. Michaelene M. Ostrosky's educational background and research focus on early childhood special education, with a particular interest in social emotional competence, social interaction and peer relationships, challenging behavior, and communication delays and disabilities. As a former teacher of young children with disabilities, Professor Ostrosky is committed to making research accessible to practitioners and family members through her writing and presentations.

Chryso Mouzourou, Ph.D., Senior Research Associate, Department of Human Sciences, College of Education and Human Ecology, The Ohio State University, 124A Mount Hall, 1050 Carmack Road, Columbus, Ohio 43210

Dr. Chryso Mouzourou's background and research focus on exploring perspectives on disabilities within communities, including families and schools, peer relationships, children's perspectives about disabilities, and cross-cultural constructions of disability as they manifest in and affect policy and practice. As a former teacher of children with diverse abilities, Professor Mouzourou is dedicated to ensuring that practitioners have access to best practices for children and their families and that her writing and teaching reflect understanding of theoretical underpinnings and current research and practice.

About the Contributors

Lisa M. van Luling, Psy.D., School Psychologist, Boston Public Schools, Behavioral Health Services, 443 Warren Street, Dorchester, Massachusetts 02121

Dr. Lisa van Luling's research interests have focused on school-based referral methods for social, emotional, and behavioral health; early childhood peer acceptance; involving families in positive behavior intervention and supports; and teacher response to teen dating violence. She is devoted to working with families and communities to support the emotional and social well-being of children and with schools to build positive school climates and student resilience and coping skills.

Lori E. Meyer, Ph.D., Assistant Professor, Department of Education, University of Vermont, 633 Main Street, Burlington, Vermont 05405

Dr. Lori Meyer's educational background, research, and teaching focus on the blending of knowledge from the fields of early childhood education and early childhood special education to meet the needs of children with diverse backgrounds and abilities in inclusive classrooms. In particular, her research is concentrated on the development of peer-related social competence among young children with or at risk for disabilities. As a former inclusive early childhood teacher, she is dedicated to increasing the use of evidence-based practices in the field of early childhood education and translating research into practice.

SeonYeong Yu, Ph.D., Assistant Professor, University of Massachusetts Amherst, 211 Furcolo Hall, 813 North Pleasant Street, Amherst, Massachusetts 01003

Dr. SeonYeong Yu's research and teaching focus on early childhood special education, with a particular interest in social inclusion, challenging behaviors, attitude development toward individuals with disabilities, and peer relationships and friendships between children with and without disabilities. As a former inclusion specialist and teacher of young children with disabilities, Professor Yu is dedicated to supporting preservice and in-service teachers as they learn and use evidence-based practices in inclusive early childhood education settings.

Hyejin Park, Ph.D., Assistant Professor, Mary Lou Fulton Teachers College, Arizona State University, 1050 South Forest Mall, Tempe, Arizona 85287

Dr. Hyejin Park's educational background, research, and teaching focus on supporting young children with disabilities in the family context, with a particular interest in public school services for children with disabilities, parent–school collaboration, and parent–child interactions. As a former special education teacher working with children with disabilities in public elementary schools and early intervention centers, she is dedicated to ensuring the use of evidence-based practices in schools and increasing parent–school collaboration.

Emily A. Dorsey, Ph.D., Assistant Professor of Practice, Department of Special Education and Communication Disorders, Barkley Memorial Center, University of Nebraska-Lincoln, PO Box 830738, Lincoln, Nebraska 68583–0738

Dr. Emily Dorsey's educational background, research interests, and teaching focus on inclusive preschool programs, with particular concentration on interagency collaboration, blended funding, and innovative service provision. She is a former early childhood special education teacher and consultant. She is invested in preservice teacher education programs and professional development opportunities for practicing teachers.

Foreword

More than any other country in the world, citizens of the United States have taken to heart the value, and indeed the virtue, of creating a society that supports "life, liberty, and the pursuit of happiness" for all its citizens. It is a fundamental belief, and nowhere has it been more evident than in the American version of the inclusion movement for children, youth, and adults with disabilities. With reference to early childhood education, the authors of this wise book note that the major professional organizations responsible for education of young children with and without disabilities have defined the key features of an inclusive program as access, participation, and support (DEC/NAEYC, 2009). The primary assumption is that through these processes, broader outcomes of social acceptance and friendships among children with different abilities will be achieved. Yet one of the most replicated findings in the field is that such acceptance for children with disabilities, and often children having other characteristics, does not occur automatically, even when access and participation occurs. *Support* is where the third leg of the three-legged inclusion stool comes into play. Support deals with the details of how to make social acceptance and social integration among children happen in educational settings. *The Making Friends Program* is one of the most valuable resources published to date that provides those necessary supports for inclusion in early childhood settings.

In *The Making Friends Program,* the authors clearly describe a process for promoting social acceptance in early childhood settings. This book has great procedural detail that teachers can follow with a high level of fidelity when applied for young children with disabilities. However, it should also be viewed as a process that extends the concepts of social acceptance and inclusion to the multidimensional features of diversity that now characterize our early childhood and early elementary programs as well as our society itself (e.g., racial, ethnic, and linguistic diversity; multiple family structures; socioeconomic circumstances). The authors very wisely begin with the teachers themselves, leading them through self-examination of their own values, perspectives, and assumptions about diversity, culture, and acceptance. We have long known that practices related to inclusion are influenced by teachers' beliefs (Lieber et al., 1998), so this process of self-discovery that leads to reflection on personal belief systems is an essential grounding for supporting social acceptance for diversity in educational settings. It is a feature of *The Making Friends Program* that is unique among curricular or instructional programs and a primary indicator that this resource is more than a "cookbook" of activities that can be picked up and used without self-reflection. It is one feature that defines this program as a process.

A strength of *The Making Friends Program* is its multicomponent approach. Understanding that acceptance, as an attitude, is built on cognitive, affective, and behavioral dimensions, and then having a coordinated set of practices that address those dimensions, is essential and is also a feature that does not appear often in procedural resources. Recognizing the literacy emphasis that is central to most early childhood education classrooms, the authors blend themes of social inclusion into literacy activities that would be a routine part of school days for young children. They then reinforce those themes through direct social interactions occurring in cooperative learning activities and solidify the themes in the home reading activities. These components have the cognitive, affective, and behavioral dimensions. From behavioral science, we know that learning and generalization occurs through participation in learning activities in multiple settings, and this certainly occurs in *The Making Friends Program*. From an educational systems perspective, the authors have highlighted features of the program aligned with the Common Core Standards. While the Common Core Standards are controversial in the current political milieu, most school systems have strategic or school-improvement plans, and the features highlighted by the authors would map well onto anticipated outcomes in those plans.

The roots of *The Making Friends Program* are in supporting social acceptance for children with disabilities in inclusive early childhood settings. The specific resources described in the literacy activities focus on issues related to disabilities, which in itself is a primary value of this resource. However, the authors clearly describe the principles of universal design and how they are embedded in *The Making Friends Program*. They provide multiple examples of ways in which the program can support social acceptance of different forms of diversity that may exist in a teacher's classroom. Teachers who are intent on supporting social acceptance of the range of diversity occurring in their classrooms could adopt the process described in this program as a central feature of their annual curriculum, incorporating the focus on different features of diversity throughout the year. Again, the "process" nature of *The Making Friends Program* could allow such adoption to happen.

Concluding on a personal note and in the spirit of full disclosure, the two primary authors and I are colleagues. The three of us arrived in the Department of Special Education at Peabody College of Vanderbilt University at the same time—they as students and I as a new assistant professor. During those years, we were fortunate to work together on the *Early Childhood Research Institute on Inclusion*, then funded by the Office of Special Education Programs (OSEP), and their contributions to that project were significant. Dr. Favazza's subsequent dissertation and then Early Career Award, also funded by OSEP, created the initial impetus for *The Making Friends Program*. The ongoing collaboration by Drs. Favazza and Ostrosky through a research project funded by the Institute of Education Science allowed the authors to develop this program into the currently well-defined procedural resource and also conduct rigorous research to examine its efficacy. I give this background to make three important points. First, the funding from these federal agencies is now paying off in very concrete ways in that *The Making Friends Program* should have an impact on the field. When looking for good investments of tax dollars, this is a primary example. Second, *The Making Friends Program* is a product of career-long programs of research, development, and scholarship in which both primary authors have engaged. It reflects decades of work with and wisdom drawn from early childhood teachers and the children in their classrooms. Third, these primary authors embrace the values of acceptance and diversity in their personal lives. They "walk the talk" in very fundamental ways.

Samuel L. Odom, Ph.D.
Frank Porter Graham Child Development Institute
University of North Carolina at Chapel Hill

Acknowledgments

There are so many colleagues and friends we would like to recognize and thank for their contributions to this book. Every step of the way, we were surrounded by people who inspired us, challenged and encouraged us, spurred us on, and celebrated successes with us. So many people came together with a shared vision to put into the hands of teachers and families an evidence-based tool to support young children, families, teachers, and school staff in their efforts to create accepting, inclusive communities for all children. None of this would have been possible without you.

First, we would like to acknowledge our incredible "dream team" who hung in there with us when asked to do myriad big and little tasks, such as developing materials; generating and entering data; interviewing children, teachers, and family members; transporting equipment and materials (including live worms!); writing and rewriting; and presenting the findings of our studies so that others might learn about the strategies reflected in this book. The dream team did all of this with impeccable professionalism, a high level of collaboration and collegiality, and a healthy dose of humor. Collectively, our team reflected the rich diversity in this book, including individuals who are biracial, are bilingual, are adopted, have special needs, have diverse ethnicities and countries of origin, and come from nontraditional homes. It was an honor to work with this wonderfully diverse team, who contributed not only to the tasks of implementing research in schools but also to the sensitivity and respect for diversity that is apparent throughout the Making Friends program. We tip our hats to the leadership provided by our five contributing coauthors; the Rhode Island research team including Kristen Fuller, Krystal Machado, Heidi Fernandez, Kelly Moroso, Jodi Kulinitch, Daniel Flynn, and Beth-Ann Tek; and the Illinois research team including Tina Brunson, Elisa Mustari, Gill Chieu, Sara Berebitsky, Elham Yaseen, Charis Price, Dalphne Ray, Corynn Cassidy, and Katie Moran.

We give a special shout-out to those who assisted with translations at various points in the process, including SeonYeong Yu, Yebon Yu, Heidi Fernandez, Alina Goncalvez Favazza, and Berkeley Hinrichs. *Muchas gracias!* 감사합니다 (*gamsahabnida*)! *Multumesc!* Ευχαριστώ (efcharistó)! In addition, we offer our thanks to the departmental faculty and staff at Rhode Island College and the University of Illinois at Urbana Champaign for their technical support and flexibility when we found ourselves juggling too many balls at one time. You enabled us to accomplish more than we thought was possible!

We owe a debt of gratitude to Dr. Joan McLaughlin at the Institute of Education Sciences in Washington, D.C. She listened intently, over and over again, to our ideas and setbacks, our successes and dreams to do more. She challenged us at each turn to rethink, dig deeper, hold the bar higher, and not give up on our belief that a sense of belonging is a worthy and cogent ideal that has an important role to play in the social and emotional success of children who are marginalized because of disabilities and differences. This book is a tribute to Joan's unwavering support of our belief that all children deserve evidence-based programs to support their success.

We extend our sincere appreciation to the editors and staff at Paul H. Brookes Publishing Co., who guided us on our voyage into the world of book publishing. They provided us with different perspectives as to how to maximize the research products and processes used in the Special Friends grant, were encouraging and patient with us in our revisions and attempts to translate research to practice, and provided a clear pathway to production and precise edits that greatly improved the quality of this book. Please know that your expertise and stellar leadership in publishing is both valued and respected.

Finally, there are hundreds of children we wish to thank, too many to name here individually, although they bring smiles to our faces as we fondly remember our interactions with them in numerous classrooms. We have often said that our greatest teachers have been the children we have had the privilege to work with on a regular basis. It was so true on this project. A huge heartfelt thanks goes out to all of the kindergarten children and their families who taught us so much about what it means to develop an understanding, acceptance, and celebration of the diversity that surrounds us. We have so many hopes and dreams that these children will show the way to many others. We thank the children and their families in our Rhode Island and Illinois communities and all of the incredible and inspiring teachers, support staff, and principals who welcomed us so graciously into their buildings and classrooms.

To our families, who simultaneously nurtured and grounded us over the years by cheering us on when we worked late into the night, listening to poignant stories from the project, bringing us coffee and tea when we rose early for conference calls, driving us to airports for countless meetings and conferences, and supporting us in many other ways. The list of small and big sacrifices they made would fill another book! Our journey would not have been possible without each of you who every day share with us your love and support. This book is for you: Poppa, Nanny, Joe, Analise, Petr, Isabella, Alina, Delroy, Cameron, George, and Danai.

Making Friends is for all those who work and play every day with the vision of creating accepting, diverse communities in all corners of the world. It is our hope that it serves as a practical resource, enabling teachers and family members to create respectful and caring communities where all individuals are welcomed and genuinely feel a sense of belonging and acceptance.

CHAPTER 1

Introduction

The Making Friends Program

TOOLBOX

- **Figure 1.1.** Hierarchy of social interactions
- **Table 1.1.** Common Core Standards
- **Table 1.2.** Anticipated benefits of the Making Friends program

---

Making Friends is a research-based program designed to promote greater acceptance of children with differences in early childhood classes (kindergarten to Grade 2). The strategies used in Making Friends align with the key components of attitude change research (Triandis, Adamopoulos, & Brinberg, 1984), which argues that "an attitude is an *idea* charged with *emotion* which predisposes a class of *actions* to a particular class of social situations" (Triandis, 1971, p. 2). Drawing on the early research on attitude change (Triandis et al., 1984), the Making Friends program utilizes home and school literacy and cooperative learning to support increased understanding and acceptance toward those with differences. Foundational information on attitudes and attitude change is discussed in greater detail in Chapter 2.

Along with the attitude change research, the Making Friends program also utilizes research on increasing the likelihood of social interactions through environmental arrangements and cooperative learning activities. Specifically, environmental arrangement strategies (e.g., selecting and rotating prosocial materials and activities, limiting materials and space; Odom & Bailey, 2001) are used in the context of cooperative learning (hands-on, small-group social activities; Beckman & Kohl, 1984; Johnson & Johnson, 1991, 1994) to support socialization among children.

Moreover, the Making Friends program is consistent with national and international responses to the increasing diversity reflected in our society (e.g., racial/ethnic, linguistic, ability, family structure) and the need for strategic efforts to support inclusion in early childhood classrooms

(DEC/NAEYC, 2009; United Nations Convention on the Rights of the Child, 1990). Making Friends was developed to ensure that all children in early childhood classrooms are accepted as full members of the inclusive classroom community.

BACKGROUND RESEARCH

In response to the growing diversity represented in early childhood classrooms (National Center for Education Statistics, 2014), federal funding pertaining to inclusion was provided to support the underlying research of the Making Friends program. The Making Friends program is based on the field-testing of Special Friends, a program designed to promote understanding and acceptance of young children with disabilities. The initial research (Favazza, LaRoe, & Odom, 1999; Favazza & Odom, 1997) in general early childhood classrooms showed the following:

The children with special needs seem a lot more comfortable . . . it looks to me like they feel like a part of the group now.
—Mr. Peter

- Most early childhood classes do not have sufficient support (e.g., information, materials, curricula) to foster accepting environments.

- Kindergartners who participated in the Special Friends program when implemented with small groups had significantly greater levels of acceptance of children with disabilities when compared to children who did not participate in the program.

A more recent study of Special Friends (Ostrosky & Favazza, 2008) examined this program as a classwide intervention in inclusive kindergarten classrooms. Because all participating classes were inclusive (as compared to previous studies, in which children with disabilities were brought into general education classrooms for intervention sessions), these classroom environments were examined to determine if supports were in place to create accepting environments (e.g., materials, information, curricula). In addition, the impact of the program on children's social skills, friendships, and acceptance of children with disabilities was examined following program implementation in kindergarten and again in the first and second grades. The program was field-tested across 4 years with 662 children from 32 kindergarten classes (16 in the Northeast, 16 in the Midwest) in a randomized control study designed to examine the efficacy of the program (16 contact control classes and 16 Special Friends classes). Research questions included the following:

1. Does participation in the program yield positive attitudes toward children with disabilities?

2. Are gains in positive attitudes maintained over time after the program ends?

3. Does participation in the classwide program yield increased social skills?

The findings were as follows:

- Preprogram sociometric ratings indicated that typically developing children were less likely to play with classmates with disabilities versus classmates without disabilities.

- Preprogram scores on a global measure of attitudes indicated that children with disabilities are generally not accepted by typically developing peers.

- *Without* intervention or intentional programming, typically developing children demonstrated increasingly negative attitudes toward children with disabilities compared to children who participated in a program designed to support acceptance of differences.

- Compared to children in control groups, children who participated in the program showed greater levels of acceptance on postprogram assessment of attitudes across 3 years. Moreover, when children's baseline (preprogram) assessment scores were taken into account, the benefits of being in the Special Friends program (e.g., sustained positive attitudes toward children with disabilities) were still evident and appeared to be accentuated 2 years after the program when compared to children who did not participate in the program. Taken together, these findings suggest that participation in Special Friends played a role in preventing children's attitudes toward individuals with disabilities from worsening over time.

- Teachers reported that children who participated in the Special Friends program demonstrated significant improvements in the areas of cooperation, assertiveness, responsibility, engagement, communication, and self-control.

- Parents and teachers reported that children's attitudes and behaviors toward peers with disabilities changed positively as a result of participation in the program, emphasizing that the program promoted greater knowledge and understanding about and acceptance of children with differing abilities.

This underlying research for the Making Friends program has relevance for all children in the current school landscape. In today's classrooms, it is more common to have a diverse group of children, such as children with disabilities, children who speak multiple languages, children who represent different races and ethnicities, and children from diverse family structures (Center for Public Education, 2012; Cox-Petersen, 2011; National Center for Education Statistics, 2014). However, as this research demonstrates, the increasing presence of diversity in classrooms does not lead to automatic acceptance. In fact, as diversity has increased in schools, so have bullying behaviors. In a noteworthy meta-analysis of 153 studies focused on bullying, researchers found that attitudes and beliefs toward those with differences, formation of social competence, early experiences of social isolation, and school climate all play a role in the development of bullying behavior (Cook, Williams, Guerra, Kim, & Sadek, 2010). Taken together, the research on bullying and the research on Special Friends point to the need for programs like this to play a preventative role during the early years by combating social isolation and negative perceptions and attitudes while simultaneously bolstering social competence and a sense of belonging in accepting class environments.

Maria increased her knowledge about how everyone is different and it's okay.
—*Mr. Gutierrez*

PHILOSOPHY

At the heart of the Making Friends program is the philosophy that all children belong; all children have a
place in early childhood and elementary classes that
celebrate differences while remembering that even in
the presence of human differences, all children are more
alike than different. Differences in race/ethnicity, ability
level, language use, and family structure are a wonderful reflection of our increasingly diverse society, and as
more diversity is represented in early childhood classrooms and schools, it is essential to implement research-based programs
like Making Friends to intentionally foster acceptance of all children.

*We learned
about sharing.
—Alyssa, 6
years old*

The idea of promoting acceptance of human differences and creating
inclusive classrooms in an increasingly diverse society is not new. Indeed,
in the United States, there is a long history of legislative attempts to form
a more inclusive society in response to pervasive attitudes of nonacceptance of differences in others. For example, two notable legislative efforts
related to the inclusion of individuals with differences were the Civil
Rights Act (PL 88-352; 1964) and the Individuals with Disabilities Education Act (IDEA; PL 94-142; 1997), formerly called the Education for All
Handicapped Children Act of 1975 (PL 94-142). The 1964 Civil Rights Act
was one of the first and most comprehensive pieces of legislation to address
discrimination in educational settings for people of color. It took years for
it to be fully implemented and another decade before similar efforts were
made on behalf of individuals with disabilities. However, many would
argue that the country still has a long way to go to fully realize this legislation for both children of color and children with disabilities.

More recently, in response to the growing number of children who are
dual language learners, each state in the United States has developed policies to protect the rights and meet the needs of children who use multiple
languages—children who are often from diverse cultures and ethnicities
(Nemeth, 2012). Likewise, a notable change in the composition of con-
temporary family structures can be seen in educational and community
settings. For example, over the past several decades, there has been an
increase in single-parent homes, same-sex parenting, and families with
adopted and/or foster children (Cox-Petersen, 2011). And whereas the
diversity in early childhood classrooms has blossomed, teachers may be
unprepared to work with children from diverse family structures or implement programs that address concerns of social isolation, nonacceptance of
others, or bullying (Kissen, 2002). In fact, there are no federal laws solely
dedicated to bullying; rather, the issue is addressed within many pieces
of legislation that were designed to protect the rights of individuals with
regard to race, national origin, color, sex, age, disability, and religion, such
as Titles IV and VI of the Civil Rights Act of 1964, Title IX of the US Education Amendments (PL 92-318; 1972), Section 504 of the Rehabilitation
Act (PL 93-112; 1973), and IDEA (Cox-Petersen, 2011).

In addition to legislative responses to the needs of diverse populations, several national and international organizations have spoken
with a singular voice about the critical need to create caring, inclusive

environments for children. For example, the position statements from the Division for Early Childhood of the Council for Exceptional Children and the National Association for the Education of Young Children (DEC/NAEYC, 2009) recommend that schools utilize evidence-based strategies to address the social and emotional needs of children by fostering a sense of belonging for all children. Fostering inclusive early childhood classes that promote a sense of belonging and acceptance of differences mirrors the sentiments of the DEC/NAEYC Joint Position Statement on Inclusion, which states, "Promoting development and belonging for every child is a widely held value among early education and intervention profession-

als and throughout our society. Early childhood inclusion is the term used to reflect these values and societal views" (DEC/NAEYC, 2009).

At the international level, the United Nations Conventions on the Rights of the Child (1990) and the Rights of Persons with Disabilities (2006) affirmed the rights of all children to live in accepting home, school, and community settings with dignity and respect for, and celebration of, their unique human differences. Both of these conventions resonate with efforts to understand and include people with different racial/ethnic backgrounds, languages, abilities, and family structures as research continues to document the numerous benefits of inclusion. These benefits include increased independence, enhanced educational outcomes and social interaction, social skill acquisition, the development of friendships, and the promotion of positive attitudes toward one another (Aboud, Mendelson, & Purdy, 2003; Fuchs & Fuchs, 1994; Hunter & Elias, 1999; Pettigrew & Tropp, 2000; Sailor, Gee, & Karasoff, 1993; Santos, Cheatham, & Duran, 2012; Waldron & McLeskey, 1998). However, even with these legislative efforts, position statements, and international conventions, social inclusion and acceptance of others does not automatically occur when children from diverse backgrounds coexist in classrooms; it requires careful and intentional efforts using research-based strategies. Making Friends is a research-based program that can be used by teachers and family members to ensure that the ideal of a caring, inclusive society becomes a reality in diverse early childhood settings.

Rylee learned that all children are the same.
—Ms. Hannon

INDICATORS OF QUALITY INCLUSION

The desired results of inclusive experiences for children with and without disabilities and their families include the following:

1. A sense of belonging and membership

2. Positive social relationships and friendship formation

3. Development and learning to reach their full potential (Catlett, Ostrosky, & Santos, 2012)

Leading early childhood professional organizations (e.g., NAEYC, DEC) name three key features of inclusion that are used to identify high-quality early childhood programs: *access, participation,* and *supports.* These three quality indices are key components of Making Friends, ensuring that it is a high-quality program aimed at promoting inclusion.

Access refers to "providing a wide range of activities and environments for every child by removing barriers and offering multiple ways to promote learning and development" (DEC/NAEYC, 2009). For example, having access to peers implies that one is socially accepted. However, research demonstrates that some children lack social acceptance (Davis, Howell, & Cook, 2002; Favazza, Phillipsen, & Kumar, 2000; Horne, 1985; Mohay & Reid, 2006; Santos, Cheatham, & Duran, 2012) if efforts are not made to raise awareness and increase understanding about children with disabilities and children from different backgrounds. Through the use of children's books and guided discussions, as presented in Making Friends, children gain a deeper understanding of differences. More importantly, however, they learn about the similarities they share with many other individuals.

Participation refers to "using a range of approaches to promote engagement in play and learning activities, and instilling a sense of belonging in every child" (DEC/NAEYC, 2009). The Making Friends program provides teachers with a variety of strategies to better support inclusion in early childhood classrooms. These strategies include ways to alter the classroom environment, improve children's levels of acceptance, and utilize children's books to optimize the learning environment. Strategies for engaging in discussions that foster understanding and acceptance *are* also included. Finally, guidelines for structuring cooperative learning activities to support social interactions and home literacy activities to involve families are also described in the program.

Supports refer to "broader aspects of the educational system such as professional development, incentives for inclusion, and opportunities for communication and collaboration among families and professionals to assure high quality inclusion" (DEC/NAEYC, 2009). Teachers play a critical role in creating a positive learning community that is welcoming to all children. Making Friends provides the background information on how attitudes are formed and specific research-based strategies to foster an accepting social climate in early childhood classes. However, efforts to promote inclusion will likely fall short unless families also are involved in meaningful ways. Materials are provided in Making Friends that engage teachers and family members in reading about differences with the explicit purpose of supporting greater understanding and social acceptance of children with disabilities, children from various racial/ethnic and linguistic backgrounds, and children with different family structures while highlighting the similarities among children (c.f., Ostrosky, Mouzourou, Favazza, & Leboeuf, 2012). In addition, each component of Making Friends (school literacy, cooperative learning groups, home literacy) includes universal design for learning (UDL)

This program helped Shannon learn about those with disabilities in a positive way.
—Ms. Skellenger

recommendations to support the engagement of all children (Mouzourou, Favazza, Ostrosky, Van Luling, 2015; Stockall, Dennis, & Miller, 2012).

PROGRAM OVERVIEW

The primary audience for Making Friends is teachers of children in kindergarten, first grade, and second grade. Secondary audiences include curriculum coordinators, school guidance counselors, social workers, inclusion coaches, and librarians. Tertiary audiences include principals and early childhood and elementary program coordinators.

While Making Friends was field-tested in kindergarten classes, the content and structure of the program lends itself to use with children in first and second grade as well. For example, 18 kindergarten-level books were selected for use with the Making Friends program using a published criterion for evaluating high-quality books about children with disabilities (Nasatir & Horn, 2003). The same criterion can be used to evaluate books about children of different racial or ethnic backgrounds, children who use different languages, or children from different family structures. The criteria for book selection are provided in Appendix 4.1, and recommendations for reviewed books are provided in Appendix 5.1.

We can play with friends with disabilities and we can learn from them.
—Bryan, 5 years old

Materials that support social interaction (Odom & Bailey, 2001) and activities that involve group effort and cooperation (Beckman & Kohl, 1984; Stoneman, Cantrell, & Hoover-Dempsey, 1983) can have a positive impact on interactions among children. Such activities were used during the initial Making Friends program to foster socialization in carefully structured cooperative learning groups. Suggestions for using these same types of materials and strategies within learning centers are included in the program.

The Making Friends program has three key components: school literacy, cooperative learning, and home literacy. Each component corresponds to one of the major influences on attitude formation and supports efforts to create accepting inclusive class environments (the link between attitude formation and each of the three components is discussed in detail in Chapter 2). Ideally, the school literacy component and cooperative learning group activities occur three times a week as teachers read and discuss stories about individuals with differences and thoughtfully organize cooperative play or cooperative learning groups where children engage in positive interactions with one another. The home literacy component occurs once a week as children select a book to take home to read and discuss with a family member (the three key components of the program are discussed in detail in Chapter 4).

Goals and Objectives

The goals of the Making Friends program are to highlight similarities between children, increase understanding of children who are different, promote acceptance, and support socialization and friendships among all children. Research-based tools that support the goals of the Making Friends program include the following:

- *Easy-to-use self-reflection exercises* to better understand how attitudes in general are formed and how childhood experiences shape early perceptions about diversity

- *A useful environmental rating tool* suitable for kindergarten through Grade 2, titled Diversity in School Environments (DSE), to examine how diversity is represented in classroom materials and curriculum

- *Resources on diversity* that may be lacking in classrooms

- *Guidelines for selecting children's books and materials* known to have high social value, as well as environmental arrangement guidelines that are likely to result in positive social outcomes for children in cooperative learning groups

- *Easy-to-follow discussion guides* that guide teachers in conversations about similarities and differences using children's literature, including tips for arranging cooperative learning groups to support socialization among children

- *Materials for involving parents and other family members* that provide opportunities to extend discussions of similarities and differences into home settings

I thought it was a wonderful addition to the kindergarten curriculum.
—Ms. Reilly

Connection to Common Core Standards

Making Friends addresses several Common Core Standards for children in kindergarten, first grade, and second grade. For example, in the category of English Language Arts and Literacy, the Common Core Standards (http://www.corestandards.org/) address the need to actively engage children in rich, culturally relevant reading experiences that reflect the diversity in their classes and cooperative learning groups that provide multiple opportunities for children to interact with one another.

- During the school literacy activities each week, children answer questions about the story details, learn new vocabulary, have opportunities to describe characters and their feelings, and connect the story content to their own life experiences.

- During the home literacy component, children have another opportunity to retell the story, use new vocabulary, and recount key ideas and events in the story as they relate the story content to family members.

- During the cooperative learning group activities, children play collaboratively with their classmates, have opportunities to problem-solve, and express their own ideas and feelings while interacting with classmates who reflect the characters in the stories.

These examples correspond to many of the Common Core Standards for reading, literature, speaking, and listening (see Table 1.1). Moreover, both

Table 1.1. Common Core Standards

Content area	Standards for kindergarten, Grade 1, and Grade 2	Making Friends component
Reading and literature	Ask and answer questions about key details Ask and answer such questions as *who, what, where, when, why,* and *how* Retell familiar stories Ask and answer questions about unknown words Use illustrations to describe characters, settings, and events Describe how characters feel Actively engage in purposeful group-reading activities	School literacy Home literacy
Speaking and listening	Participate in collaborative conversations Follow agreed-on rules for discussions Confirm understanding of text read aloud Recount details of key ideas Speak audibly, expressing thoughts and feelings Describe people and events, and express ideas	School literacy Home literacy Cooperative learning
Math	Respect others (e.g., listen carefully) Understand others' points of view and perspectives Identify social cues (verbal and physical) to determine how others feel Predict others' feelings and reactions Manage and express emotions in relationships, respecting diverse viewpoints	Cooperative learning School literacy Home literacy

the Common Core Standards and the Making Friends program address several social and emotional skills, which correlate with developmentally appropriate practices (Fox & Lentini, 2006). For example, within the Common Core Standards for math, the following skills are addressed and supported though the cooperative learning and literacy components of Making Friends: respecting others and diverse viewpoints, understanding others' points of view and perspectives, recognizing social cues to determine how others feel, predicting others' feelings, and expressing emotions in relationships.

Other social competencies that are supported in the Making Friends program include skills such as following rules, routines, and directions; identifying feelings of self and others; sharing materials; taking turns; and expressing empathy for others. All of these skills reflect elements of the social environment and are critical to creating a caring, inclusive community of learners. These same social skills are consistent with the hierarchy of promoting social interaction and social competence among young children described by Brown, Odom, and Conroy (2001; see Figure 1.1). While the Making Friends program provides opportunities for understanding differences in early childhood classes through literacy and cooperative learning activities, teachers are encouraged to collaborate with families by sending literacy activities home with their children. Research has shown that promoting an understanding of human differences and enlisting family involvement are essential features in high-quality inclusive early childhood classes (Christian, 2006; Diamond & Innes, 2001). By examining the Common Core Standards in Table 1.1 and the hierarchy of social interactions in Figure 1.1, it should be evident that Making Friends addresses young children's literacy and learning needs while also addressing key social and emotional learning needs reflected in the math Common Core Standards. These skills are addressed through developmentally

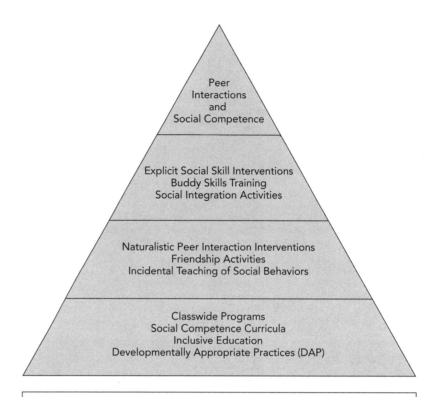

Figure 1.1.   Hierarchy of social interactions. (From Brown, W. H., Odom, Samuel, L., Conroy, M. A. [2001]. *An Intervention Hierarchy for Promoting Young Children's Peer Interactions in Natural Environments.* Topics in Early Childhood Special Education Vol. 21 [3] pp.162–175. Copyright © 2001 by Topics in Early Childhood Special Education. Reprinted by permission of SAGE Publications, Inc.)

appropriate activities including reading/circle time, cooperative learning, and home reading.

In summary, the Making Friends program fills a critical gap in early childhood programs by presenting research-based strategies known to support an understanding of similarities and differences. Strategies for evaluating the social climate of classrooms, suggestions for books and materials to use in early childhood settings, and specific suggestions for structuring cooperative learning groups to foster social interactions are provided.

ANTICIPATED BENEFITS

The Making Friends program was developed to support schools in creating inclusive communities of learners and a sense of belonging for all children. To this end, the anticipated benefits for teachers, children, and families include the following (and are summarized in Table 1.2):

Table 1.2. Anticipated benefits of the Making Friends program

Children	Teachers	Families
Increased understanding about similarities and differences Increased acceptance of all children Increased friendships among children Additional opportunities for literacy at school and with family	Increased knowledge of the attitude construct Increased knowledge about how to discuss similarities and differences with children Increased knowledge about how to select high-quality books and materials to support social acceptance and socialization among children	Increased understanding about similarities and differences Increased knowledge about how to discuss similarities and differences with children Additional opportunities to engage in reading at home with their children

We can play with friends with disabilities and we can learn from them.
—Bryan, 5 years old

- Teachers will learn strategies for evaluating their classroom environment and strategies that support their efforts to create a positive inclusive climate and community of learners.

- Teachers and family members will partner in shared book reading activities at school and home focusing on books about children with linguistic differences, disabilities, varied racial/ethnic backgrounds, and varied family structures.

- Teachers and family members will gain increased knowledge about how to talk about differences while also highlighting and celebrating similarities.

- Children will gain a better understanding of human differences and similarities.

- Children will increase their level of acceptance of children with disabilities, linguistic differences, diverse racial/ethnic backgrounds, and diverse family structures.

- Children will gain skills that contribute to social and emotional development and skill areas from Common Core Standards in reading and math.

While field-testing the Making Friends program, careful attention was given to the feedback gathered from children, teachers, and family members who participated in the research. Indeed, participants in the Making Friends program found it beneficial, with teachers noting many positive outcomes among children in their classrooms, including greater understanding of one another, improved capacity to play, increased acceptance, and new friendships. Family members also found the literacy-based program beneficial for their children, citing enjoyment of high-quality books, useful conversations between family members and children, and new knowledge about how to talk with their children about similarities and differences.

Because some children are at risk of being rejected in early childhood settings without support to foster acceptance among children in diverse class settings (Aboud, Mendelson, & Purdy, 2003; Bricker, 1995; Favazza & Odom, 1996, 1997; Favazza, Phillipsen, & Kumar, 2000; Hunter & Elias,

1999; Pettigrew & Tropp, 2000; Sailor et al., 1993), teachers and family members cannot take a "wait and see" approach. Rather, they must actively participate in the development of an accepting community within their early childhood settings and at home. The Making Friends program is an important step in creating that sense of belonging for all children in our increasingly diverse society.

CHAPTER 2

Attitudes

TOOLBOX

Figure 2.1. Components of an attitude

Figure 2.2. Connection of the components of Making Friends to attitude influences

Figure 2.3. The basics of attitude formation

Figure 2.4. Strategies that promote accepting attitudes

As mentioned in Chapter 1, the Making Friends program uses attitude change research (Triandis, Adamopoulos, & Brinberg, 1984) as a foundation to create accepting multicultural inclusive classes. Therefore, this chapter provides more in-depth information on attitudes, including the definition of an attitude, developmental information on how and when attitudes are formed, a brief summary of research findings on attitudes, and implications for teachers and family members. For the seminal research on attitudes and attitude development, see Allport (1935). For more recent research on attitudes and attitude change, see Ajzen (2001), Wood and Fabrigar (2012), Yu and Ostrosky (2012), and Yu, Ostrosky, and Fowler (2012).

WHAT IS AN ATTITUDE?

While there are many ways of defining an attitude, the Making Friends program is based on one of the early definitions: "an attitude is an *idea* charged with *emotion* which predisposes a class of *actions* to a particular class of social situations" (Triandis, 1971, p. 2). Notably, attitudes are complex, with a *cognitive* component (ideas and thoughts), an *affective* component (feelings), and a *behavioral* component (behavioral intentions, behavior or actions toward/away from the attitude referent; Ajzen, 1988; Eagly & Chaiken, 1993; Triandis, 1971). In this case, the attitude referent would be a child who is different from oneself. Each component of an

We enjoyed, as a family, reading books each week.
—Ms. Eacott

attitude generates something different: ideas and thoughts (he or she is bad or good, or like or unlike me), feelings (like/dislike, enjoyment/discomfort, anxiety/calm), and behaviors or behavioral intentions (to avoid or seek out). See Figure 2.1.

HOW ARE ATTITUDES FORMED?

Attitudes are formed over time by many influences that begin occurring when a child is very young. Simply put, children learn attitudes. Attitudes do not just happen; attitudes are encouraged and supported in particular directions (toward or away; positive or negative) by three primary sources: indirect experiences, direct experiences, and the child's primary social group (Derman-Sparks, Tanaka Higa, & Sparks, 1980; Triandis, 1971; Triandis, Adamopoulos, & Brinberg, 1984). Let's take a look at each source that influences attitude development.

I noticed during play centers that children without disabilities were more encouraging to friends who needed help.
—Ms. Muwana

Indirect Experiences

There are many indirect experiences or sources of information that shape attitudes by indirectly providing information. These include but are not limited to how individuals are portrayed in books, movies, television, photographs, and conversations. Each of these sources of information indirectly informs a child's sense of self and sense of others. Stated another way, each of these sources of information provides both a mirror (shaping perceptions of self) and a window (shaping perceptions of others; Blaska, 2000). Therefore, children are indirectly exposed to the attitude referent (e.g., child with disabilities, child from a different race or ethnicity, child who uses multiple languages, child who is from a diverse family structure) through the information they receive in print and visual media or through conversations in daily life. Over time, the collection of these indirect experiences plays a role in shaping the development of positive or negative attitudes. Here are three examples that illustrate the influence of indirect experiences:

- If a person is *not portrayed at all* in conversations, books, or popular media, this sends a strong and silent message that such a person is excluded, invisible, or does not belong (Blaska, 2000; Hughes, Rodriguez, Smith, Johnson, Stevenson, & Spicer, 2006). This is easy to see when you consider how people of color, people with disabilities, single-parent families, and people from diverse cultural backgrounds historically were not evident in books, television, and movies.

Figure 2.1.   Components of an attitude.

- If a person is *repeatedly portrayed in a negative light* in conversations, books, movies, television, or video games (e.g., a character with a disability or a character from a specific ethnic or racial group is often the "villain") or is portrayed in ways that emphasize that he or she belongs to a different world (e.g., only Caucasian characters succeed, only Latino or African American characters live in poverty), it can predispose children to have a stereotypic view, to be less accepting, or to espouse negative attitudes toward others. For example, there are many characters with disabilities from animated movies that are portrayed as the "villain," excluded from society, or ridiculed, such as Captain Hook in *Peter Pan*, the Hunchback of Notre Dame, Dumbo the Elephant, and Scar from *The Lion King*. While these movies may be viewed as entertainment for young children, they also convey subtle and often stereotypic messages of nonacceptance of those who are different (Hunt, 1991). Likewise, stereotypic and negative portrayals of Latino and African American characters in the media are well documented, which many speculate contributes to nonacceptance of individuals from diverse racial and ethnic groups (Dixon & Linz, 2000; Mastro, Behm-Morawitz, & Kopacz, 2008). These realities point to the need for informed conversations about diversity *representation* in the media (Vittrup & Holden, 2010).

- If a person is *repeatedly portrayed in a positive light* in conversations, books, movies, television, or video games (e.g., a Spanish-speaking child has friends, a child with two moms is happy and well loved) and is portrayed in everyday situations that demonstrate similarities with others (e.g., liking music and dancing, struggling with homework), this provides a positive narrative or sends a positive message that can predispose children to be more accepting (Jordan & Hernandez-Reif, 2009). Even the simple use of modeling positive behaviors (e.g., playing with toys that represent children from diverse racial and ethnic groups) or presenting positive color–word associations (e.g., "The black doll is beautiful just like you.") can serve as a positive catalyst for changing children's preferences and attitudes (Powell-Hopson & Hopson, 1992).

I learned sign language!
—*Jorge, 6½ years old*

William [a child with a disability] was very welcomed back after his weeklong absence for surgery.
—*Mrs. Cronin*

Direct Experiences

A similar thing happens with direct experiences. Direct experiences are authentic, firsthand encounters with individuals who are different in some way. These experiences may include playing with a child with disabilities, a child who speaks another language, a child who is racially or ethnically different, or a child from a home with a unique family structure (e.g., raised by adoptive parents, two dads, or a grandmother).

- If repeated experiences and/or interactions with others who are different from one's self are negative, uncomfortable, or unsuccessful, this will likely have a negative impact on early perceptions, setting the stage for negative attitudes.

- If repeated experiences and/or interactions with individuals who are diverse are positive, comfortable, or successful, it will likely have a positive impact on early perceptions, setting the stage for positive attitudes (Aboud, Mendelson, & Purdy, 2003).

Students are playing much better together; they're cooperating.
—Ms. Amaya

Primary Social Group

Last, a child's primary social group greatly influences the attitudes that he or she adopts (Castelli, Zogmaister, & Tomelleri, 2009; Hughes et al., 2006; Jeynes, 2005; Peretti & Sydney, 1984; Sinclair, Dunn, & Lowery, 2005; Thornton & Camburn, 1987; Weinraub, Clemens, Sockloff, Ethridge, Gracely, & Myers, 1984). Families are the first primary social group for young children, and consequently, parents and other family members play a critical role in the development of perceptions and attitude formation.

- If family members make disparaging remarks about an individual of another race, a young child will learn to do the same.

- If a child is cared for by a relative who repeatedly demonstrates pity and discomfort when in the presence of children with disabilities, the child will likely do the same, mirroring the actions and words they have seen or heard.

- If family members show excitement and enthusiasm about their new neighbors who speak another language, the child will most likely mirror their behavior.

However, it is also important to realize that as children age, the social group expands to include teachers and peers (Horne, 1985; Jones, 1984; Wood & Fabrigar, 2012). Because of this, it is not surprising when children espouse new or different attitudes of acceptance or rejection as they become increasingly influenced by the words and actions of their teachers and later their peers. So it is important to include family members, teachers, and peers in programs that promote acceptance and inclusion and to ensure that these programs are ongoing, matching the ongoing nature of attitude development.

While attitudes are influenced by indirect experiences, direct experiences, and the primary social group, the strength of these attitudes is dependent on *how often children receive those positive or negative messages* and the *reinforcement* (praise, feedback, feelings of pleasure) they receive from espousing the attitudes (e.g., saying and doing positive things with someone with a disability or

Our whole family participated in these activities and really enjoyed it.
—Ms. McQuaid

an individual of a different race). If a child is praised or applauded for his or her actions, it is likely that the actions will increase or persist. For example, if a child is emboldened by his peers' attention and applause when bullying a child who is of a different ethnic background or who has disabilities, the behavior is reinforced, and the negative attitudes are strengthened. Both the reinforcement associated with actions and words and the frequency of positive and negative messages associated with the direct and indirect experiences and the social group can strengthen attitudes. Finally, it is worth pointing out that while attitudes can change, the longer a person has a particular attitude, the more difficult it may be to change the patterns of thoughts and feelings (internal narratives) and the patterns of behavior.

WHEN DOES ATTITUDE FORMATION ABOUT HUMAN DIFFERENCES BEGIN?

[I noticed children] trying to help each other and helping students with disabilities when having difficulties.
—Ms. Santos

The presence of negative attitudes toward individuals who are different from oneself is not a new phenomenon, nor is it a phenomenon seen only in the United States. There is a long history of negative perceptions and attitudes toward people with disabilities, which date back to ancient Greek and Roman times (Munyi, 2012) and are still widespread. Likewise, there is a long history of nonacceptance and discrimination related to race. Many would say that racism originated with the slave trade as slaveholders from Rome and Greece created and perpetuated the belief that slavery was natural because Africans were not human beings (Taylor, 2000). Likewise, there is extensive research on attitudes toward individuals who speak different languages, with studies demonstrating that attributes such as competence, attractiveness, and personal integrity are assigned to individuals based on the language they speak or their accent (Baker & Jones, 1989). Finally, in recent years, attention has focused on the increasing numbers of children from nontraditional families who have encountered nonacceptance or bullying in school settings (Bliss & Harris, 1998; Fitzgerald, 1999; Lamme & Lamme, 2002).

However, new research sheds light on the challenge of promoting acceptance of differences in young children. Children under 2 years of age already show preferences toward those whom they perceive as similar to themselves, even if the child who is similar to them engages in inappropriate or aggressive behaviors (Hamlin, Mahajan, Liberman, & Wynn, 2013). Infants and toddlers demonstrate a preference for others who match their preferences in choice of toys, food, and clothing (Fawcett & Markson, 2010; Manhajan & Wynn, 2012). As children age, ideas about differences become more established, and positive or negative behaviors in the presence of differences become common patterns depending on how family members and teachers respond to natural human differences. For example, by age 3, children notice gender differences in other children and begin forming early perceptions of as well as preferences for those who are the same gender. By age 4, early perceptions of race or skin tone are being formed, and by age 5, early perceptions of children with disabilities are formed (Derman-Sparks & ABC Task Force, 1989; Gerber, 1977; Jones & Sisk, 1970).

These early perceptions are the beginning of attitude formation, and the strength and direction (positive or negative) of the attitude will depend on how it is influenced by the child's social group and the direct and indirect experiences he or she has. Moreover, there is a fundamental relationship between peer acceptance and children's socialization and full membership in early childhood classes. For example, children with disabilities are often assigned lower social status by their typically developing peers and are also nominated less frequently as friends (Dyson, 2005; Favazza, Phillipsen, & Kumar, 2000; Nowicki, & Sandieson, 2002; Yu, Ostrosky, & Fowler, 2014). Using evidence-based strategies to intentionally promote greater understanding and acceptance of children who are different is a critical step in efforts to create classrooms that are welcoming and supportive of all children. See Figure 2.2, which illustrates how the components of the Making Friends program connect to the attitude construct.

WHAT ARE THE IMPLICATIONS FOR PRACTICE?

Research has consistently demonstrated that teachers and family members have a powerful impact on children's attitudes. In fact, every day, teachers and family members communicate their attitudes about a myriad of people, events, and situations to children through the ways they talk about others or answer questions, the ways they behave, and the ways they show approval or disapproval of children's actions and words (Innes & Diamond,

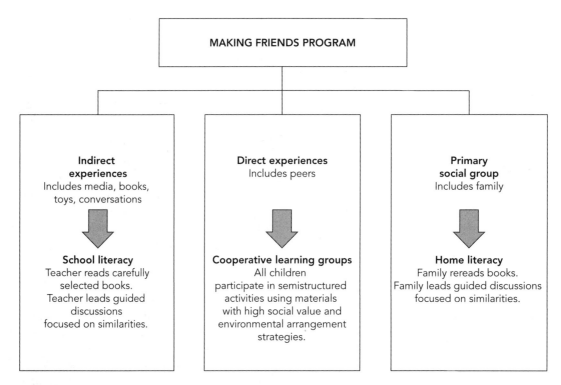

Figure 2.2. Connection of the components of Making Friends to attitude influences.

1999; Lieber, Capell, Sandall, Wolfberg, Horn, & Beckman, 1998; Park & Ostrosky, 2013). So what can be done to ensure that attitudes of acceptance are developed in children? The following things are important to consider:

- *Knowing oneself and one's own attitudes.* Before beginning the Making Friends program, it is important that all adults involved understand how attitudes are formed and have a clear sense of their own attitudes (Garman, 2005). In Chapter 3, exercises are provided to enable participants in the Making Friends program to reflect on their own attitudes and understand the early influences on these attitudes (i.e., indirect experiences, direct experiences, and messages received from parents and other family members). It is important to take time to think about these components of the attitude construct and reflect on how to model attitudes of acceptance for all children.

- *Using a multicomponent approach.* It is important to keep in mind that an attitude is a multicomponent concept that is influenced by indirect experiences, direct experiences, and the child's primary social group, which are addressed in the Making Friends program through school literacy, cooperative learning groups, and home literacy, respectively. Previous research has demonstrated that addressing all three components of the attitude construct is more effective in promoting attitudinal change than addressing any single component (Favazza, Phillipsen, & Kumar, 2000). In addition, attitudes are multidimensional in nature, reflecting one's feelings, ideas, and behaviors. Therefore, it is important that these aspects of attitudes are reflected in conversations with children and that all components of the Making Friends program are implemented to optimize the outcomes.

- *Being a discriminating consumer.* All environments and the materials and activities in these environments influence children; therefore, it is important that environments are examined to maximize the positive influences in classrooms and the overall school setting. In Chapter 3, a checklist is provided for teachers to evaluate their school and class setting to ensure that the environment, materials, media, and activities in which children are engaged reflect others in positive ways and support conversations about the wonderful and unique ways people are different and the surprising ways in which people are all more alike than different. It is recommended that teachers and family members utilize these and other resources to infuse a positive perspective about the diverse world in which we live.

- *Involving family members, especially when children make the transition into a new class.* In this highly mobile world, children make the transition into new educational settings on a fairly regular basis. It is important that teachers partner with family members to ease these transitions. Before a child arrives in a new class, teachers can think about ways to create positive connections for all children (Favazza, 1998). For example, teachers can have conversations with their students about the arrival of a new friend. In addition, teachers can engage in conversations with the new child and family members so as to prepare them for the new class and convey excitement about the new adventure. Research has demonstrated that parents and other family members have a powerful impact on children's attitudes toward differences and that children will often follow the lead provided by their family members and teachers (Castelli, Zogmaister, & Tomelleri, 2009; Jeynes, 2005; Peretti & Sydney, 1984; Sinclair, Dunn, & Lowery, 2005; Thornton & Camburn, 1987; Weinraub et al., 1984). Therefore, it is important to involve family members when a new child enters the class and throughout the Making Friends program.

My favorite book was Deaf Musicians; *when you are deaf, you can't hear, but you can use sign language.*
—Shawn

- *Planning for maintenance of an accepting, welcoming, and inclusive setting.* Because children are continually influenced by the world in which they live, it is important to use Making Friends as an ongoing program that welcomes conversations and promotes acceptance and a sense of belonging. In doing so, children are more likely to be predisposed to be more accepting of the wonderful diversity that surrounds them (Siraj-Blatchford & Clarke, 2000; see also TeachingForChange.org).

Finally, in response to increasing diversity, the National Association for the Education of Young Children developed a position statement to guide

---

Attitudes are complex, multicomponent cognitive structures.
Attitudes include *ideas, feelings,* and *behaviors.*

The attitudes of younger children are more malleable than those of older children and adults.
Teachers and family members can affect the formation of attitudes with careful attention to *indirect experiences, direct experiences,* and the *child's primary social group.*

Attitudes are relatively stable once they are formed.
Resistance to attitude change as one grows older is a reflection of this stability. Because of this, it is important to intervene during the early childhood years.

Without effective programs in place that are intentionally designed to promote acceptance of differences, significant change in levels of acceptance is less likely.
Infants, toddlers, and preschoolers typically show preferences for others that they perceive as similar to themselves. Because of this, young children need the influential adults in their lives to provide intentional and positive conversations and activities that model acceptance of human differences.

Figure 2.3. The basics of attitude formation. (*Sources:* Favazza & Odom, 1996, 1997; Favazza, Phillipsen, & Kumar, 2000.)

Indirect Experiences

Intentional and ongoing use of . . .
Positive, strength-based language in daily conversation
Posters and signage in the environment
Inclusive, multicultural, multilingual materials and media in the environment
Carefully selected books with guided discussions

Direct Experiences

Authentic and carefully planned use of . . .
Structured and supported play opportunities
Environmental arrangements
Paired buddies and heterogeneous groups
Making Friends program during school
Inclusive after-school activities

Child's Primary Social Group

Thoughtful and inclusive . . .
Teacher training and participation in the Making Friends program
Parent training and participation in the Making Friends program
Implementation of the Making Friends program for all children

---

Figure 2.4. Strategies that promote accepting attitudes.

practitioners as they strive to create more inclusive and welcoming early childhood classrooms (NAEYC, 1995). The strategies suggested in this book are consistent with this position statement. A summary of key points from this chapter is found in Figures 2.3 and 2.4; these summaries can be used with teachers and family members when starting the Making Friends program.

CHAPTER 3

Reflective Exercises

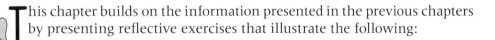

This chapter builds on the information presented in the previous chapters by presenting reflective exercises that illustrate the following:

1. How early experiences shape early perceptions, which, if consistently reinforced over time, influence ideas, feelings, and behaviors that converge to form an attitude

2. How the culture in which one lives influences attitude development through indirect experiences, direct experiences, and one's primary social group (family)

3. How these same attitudinal components (ideas, feelings, and behaviors) and influences (indirect experiences, direct experiences, and primary social group) affect attitudes toward people from diverse backgrounds

The reflective exercises detailed throughout this chapter will help you think about how your early life experiences led to early perceptions associated with those experiences:

- The Attitude Exercise demonstrates the three components of an attitude: ideas, feelings, and behaviors.

- The Remember Who You Are exercise demonstrates the three primary influences on attitude development that occur within a broader cultural context through indirect experiences, direct experiences, and your primary social group.

- The Unpack Your Perceptions About Diversity exercise applies the three components of an attitude and the three influences on attitude development to perceptions about people from diverse backgrounds.

In addition, teachers are encouraged to use two tools prior to implementing the Making Friends program: the Diversity in School Environments exercise and the Making Friends Vignettes.

So far, Lin Rose has had a great experience with seeing her uncle in a wheelchair. She has gotten rides and sees that even though Uncle Errol is in a wheelchair, he can do a lot of things a nonhandicapped person can do. For instance, he is married with children, drives a car, and is an avid wheelchair rugby and basketball player.
—*Mr. Lee**

- The Diversity in School Environments (DSE) exercise is used to evaluate an early childhood environment to determine if other items are needed within the class or school environment to reflect diversity with regard to disability, race/ethnicity, language, or family structure. The items on the DSE require one to examine the visual and aesthetic environment, classroom curriculum, classroom books, materials in the dramatic play area, classroom language such as labels on shelves, and items that are found in the broader school environment.

- The Making Friends Vignettes provide brief scenarios for each diversity area addressed in the Making Friends program. The purpose of the vignettes is to support teachers in "thinking on their feet" when a conversation is overheard or a behavior is observed that shows misunderstanding and/or nonacceptance. The vignettes provide opportunities to think about how one might respond to these naturally occurring situations among children, and in doing so, they prepare teachers with simple ways of responding to children that will lead to greater understanding and acceptance of and socialization among children.

---

*The terminology used in these quotations reflects the terms used in local settings. When using the Making Friends program, it is important to use current person-first terminology, such as "a person without disabilities" instead of "a nonhandicapped person."

The exciting news is that attitudes can be shaped and changed in a positive direction if family members and teachers understand how early perceptions shape later attitudes, examine the ways in which they contribute to children's attitude development, and work together during the early childhood years to ensure that the course of attitude formation for children takes a positive and accepting direction. The exercises in this chapter set the stage for early positive attitude formation before proceeding to Chapter 4, which provides details for structuring the Making Friends program to intentionally and effectively promote acceptance.

THE ATTITUDE EXERCISE

In Chapter 2, we noted that an attitude has three interconnected components: a cognitive component (thoughts or ideas), an affective component (feelings), and a behavioral component (actions or behaviors). The Attitude Exercise incorporates these three components in a series of questions to illustrate how one's personal experiences can influence ideas, feelings, and behaviors, which, if repeatedly reinforced over time, become a more permanent, cohesive multicomponent attitude. The Attitude Exercise should be completed individually. However, several people who work together within a classroom or on a team (e.g., teachers, speech language pathologists, student teachers, social workers) can use it as part of a group discussion. If it is to be discussed within a group, it is recommended that each person first complete the Attitude Exercise individually before responses are shared with the group.

The Attitude Exercise includes several questions about an early childhood experience (an event or situation) that was either very positive or very negative. The respondent is asked to describe his or her early ideas, feelings, and behaviors associated with the situation/event and asked to explain who or what reinforced these ideas, feelings, and behaviors that eventually cemented, forming a long-held attitude.

The following examples (Figures 3.1–3.4) represent how four people responded to this exercise. When reading through these examples, think about the similarities across the four responses. Note that these examples are intentionally focused on attitudes associated with general situations or events (math, new experiences, eating vegetables, gardening). These

Similar to last week, our students with disabilities have friends in the room, who save spots on the rug for them and share with them.
—Ms. Bentz

Attitude Exercise

Directions: Identify an experience from your early childhood years that focused on an event, situation, or item that led you to have an early positive or negative perception and that over time shaped your attitude toward or against the event, situation, or item. Then answer the following questions:

1. What do you have a positive or negative attitude about?
2. What or who influenced, promoted, or led you to having that attitude?
3. What were your *thoughts/ideas* about the event, item, or situation?
4. How did you *feel?* What were your *emotions or sensations?*
5. How was your *behavior* changed or altered because of that experience? How *did you act or what did you do* in this situation or event / in the presence of this item?

Attitude Exercise: Cathy

Directions: Identify an experience from your childhood that focused on an event, situation, or item that led you to have an early positive or negative perception and that over time shaped your attitude toward or against the event, situation, or item. Then answer the following questions:

1. What do you have a positive or negative attitude about?

   I have a negative attitude toward math.

2. What or who influenced, promoted, or lead you to having that attitude?

   My third grade teacher stood me in front of class almost every day to count money. Because I could not count money, I was embarrassed as I stood in front of everyone.

3. What were your *thoughts/ideas* about the event, item, or situation?

   I thought I was dumb. However, today, I have different thoughts. I think teachers need to be more sensitive so as not to embarrass children in front of others.

4. How did you *feel*? What were your *emotions or sensations*?

   I felt embarrassed and cried before going to school on the days that we were having oral drills on math problems.

5. How was your *behavior* changed or altered because of that experience? How *did you act or what did you do* in this situation or event / in the presence of this item?

   I begged to stay home, and if that did not work, I would hide in the bathroom. Later in my life, I often delayed balancing my checkbook because I was worried I would make mistakes. For years, I avoided math classes, even in college. Finally, a math professor asked me why I was so negative toward mathematics. When I explained the reason, he apologized for the teacher. Then, amazingly, he went on to explain that I was actually quite good at math.

Figure 3.1.   Cathy's attitude toward math.

Attitude Exercise: Beck

Directions: Identify an experience from your childhood that focused on an event, situation, or item that led you to have an early positive or negative perception and that over time shaped your attitude toward or against the event, situation, or item. Then answer the following questions:

1. What do you have a positive or negative attitude about?

   I have a positive attitude toward people, places, experiences, or foods that are different and new.

2. What or who influenced, promoted, or lead you to having that attitude?

   We moved often when I was a child, and before we moved, my parents always said, with great excitement, "We are going on another grand adventure!" They would pull out maps so we could see where we were going and check out library books to learn about the new places and people. When we arrived, they would make a big deal out of trying new foods, wearing different clothing, or learning new languages or new vocabulary, introducing us to the new and different people around us. They painted a picture that each move was going to be exciting and made sure it was.

3. What were your *thoughts/ideas* about the event, item, or situation?

   I thought new experiences were cool and wonderful. I thought different people were exotic. It made me think of surprises, discoveries of new foods, different types of houses and ways of life. It was not always easy, but the overriding message was that we have a lot to learn and experience from the differences in others.

4. How did you *feel?* What were your *emotions or sensations?*

   I felt excited, fascinated, intrigued, and challenged. And I still feel excited when traveling to new places or meeting someone who is different or who has a different life experience. Really!

5. How was your *behavior* changed or altered because of that experience? How *did you act or what did you do* in this situation or event / in the presence of this item?

   As a child, at recess, I looked for other children who were different from me, kids who were of another race or ethnicity, spoke another language, or had a disability. I read books about people from different countries and cultures. I still try new foods or clothing and revel in hearing new ways of looking at the world; espousing the same sense of adventure given to me early in life.

Figure 3.2. Beck's attitude toward new experiences.

Attitude Exercise: Sharon

Directions: Identify an experience from your childhood that focused on an event, situation, or item that led you to have an early positive or negative perception and that over time shaped your attitude toward or against the event, situation, or item. Then answer the following questions:

1. What do you have a positive or negative attitude about?

    I have a negative attitude about vegetables, but it all started with broccoli!

2. What or who influenced, promoted, or lead you to having that attitude?

    When I was very young, I liked broccoli. One day, I decided I did not want to eat my broccoli. But one of my parents decided that I must eat everything that was on my plate. When I declined, I either sat at the table until the broccoli was gone (eaten, hidden in my pocket, given to the dog), or it reappeared the next morning, hidden in my pancakes! This is a true story! Soon I generalized my disdain for broccoli to other vegetables, especially green ones.

3. What were your *thoughts/ideas* about the event, item, or situation?

    I thought, even as a child, that I should be allowed to choose what I like and dislike, and I thought that only I knew whether I was hungry or not. Nobody else can know that, right? I grew up with firm ideas about this common dinnertime dilemma. I still think that children should be encouraged to try new foods, but they should be allowed to have preferences.

4. How did you *feel*? What were your *emotions or sensations*?

    Before dinner, when I smelled the broccoli cooking, I had feelings of dread. To this day, I still feel nauseous (sick) at the smell of broccoli cooking.

5. How was your *behavior* changed or altered because of that experience? How *did you act or what did you do* in this situation or event / in the presence of this item?

    I generalized my disdain for broccoli to all green vegetables: asparagus, brussels sprouts, and spinach. I would never buy, cook, or eat most veggies. Broccoli is my husband's favorite food, but he agreed to cook it when I am away. Years later, I tasted okra, green beans, zucchini, and many different vegetables, and I loved them! But this change took a long time.

Figure 3.3.   Sharon's attitude toward vegetables.

Attitude Exercise: Matt

Directions: Identify an experience from your childhood that focused on an event, situation, or item that led you to have an early positive or negative perception and that over time shaped your attitude toward or against the event, situation, or item. Then answer the following questions:

1. What do you have a positive or negative attitude about?

   I have a very positive attitude about gardening.

2. What or who influenced, promoted, or lead you to having that attitude?

   My father traveled a lot when I was a child, but when he was home, he was always in our garden, weeding, planting, and harvesting the crops that fed our family. Some of my fondest memories are of watching Dad get excited about the new plants we were going to grow. And while we did the hard work of digging, planting, weeding, watering, harvesting, and repairing the fencing, he would make up games, so the time would pass by quickly. And the food from the garden ended up on our dinner table, or we would give away all the extra food to those who needed it.

3. What were your *thoughts/ideas* about the event, item, or situation?

   I thought gardening was an awesome, fun activity. Because my father was away often, the time spent with him seemed precious. We had work to do when he was home, but because of his enthusiasm and game-like approach, I grew to appreciate my time with him, and his excitement about gardening became contagious.

4. How did you *feel*? What were your *emotions or sensations*?

   I loved the smell of fresh overturned dirt, planting and harvesting crops. I got excited when planting season arrived and felt a great sense of pride at growing our own food; I enjoyed cooking with veggies from our garden. I still have special feelings about gardening with my father. Just the smell of warm overturned dirt brings to mind fond memories.

5. How was your *behavior* changed or altered because of that experience? How *did you act or what did you do* in this situation or event / in the presence of this item?

   I plant every year. I love to dig in dirt, plant things, watch them grow, and tell stories to my children about the games my father used to play to enlist our help in the garden. My wife and I cook with fresh fruits and vegetables as well. I learned to make games out of the chores I do with my kids so the tasks are fun, and I developed the habit of giving away the extra food.

Figure 3.4. Matt's attitude toward gardening.

real-life examples are provided to enable the respondent to first reflect on attitudes about relatively neutral, less personal topics before using the same exercise to focus on more personal attitudes toward a specific population (individuals with disabilities, racial/ethnic differences, linguistic differences, or diverse family structures).

What Can Be Learned from These Responses to the Attitude Exercise?

Determine some of the components of an attitude that are evident across all four responses to the Attitude Exercise. What else stands out across these responses?

- Perceptions about human differences begin to take shape in the early experiences of young children.

- Family members and teachers are very influential in shaping a child's early perceptions, especially if the experience is repeated with the same or a consistent outcome over time (such as a repeated positive experience or a repeated negative experience).

- How teachers and family members respond to early experiences shape perceptions, which over time can grow into attitudes that are based on firm ideas, genuine feelings, and actions toward or against the attitude referent.

- Some early perceptions are generalized to other people or events. For example, Sharon's perceptions about broccoli were generalized to other green vegetables; Matt's perceptions about one chore generalized to other chores; Beck's perceptions about embracing novel experiences (places, foods) generalized to other new experiences.

Now, before completing the Attitude Exercise, there are a few important points to remember to maximize the outcome of the exercise.

1. The Attitude Exercise is most meaningful when the respondent uses real-life situations from the early childhood years. Because this may take some thought as to which event or situation to use for the exercise, it is best to first discuss this set of suggestions with colleagues or others using the Making Friends program and then take some time to think about the questions before responding to them.

2. When completing the Attitude Exercise, it is important to remember that discussing one's attitudes can be a difficult activity for some individuals, as it involves recalling personal events that may trigger strong, emotional responses about events or situations that profoundly influenced a person's life. Likewise, hearing

Alexander enjoyed this book and realized a disability is not a reason to miss out on enjoyable activities.
—Ms. Finnigan

about the attitude development journey of others may be challenging, especially if their attitudes are different. Because of this, prior to undertaking this exercise with colleagues (in a group setting), it is important to stress that responses should be expressed and discussions undertaken in ways that are respectful and sensitive to all. A safe environment for discussing attitudes must be created.

3. It is important to first use the examples of attitudes about general situations to facilitate a more lighthearted conversation before easing into discussions about more personal situations involving specific populations of individuals. Using the examples provided previously (attitudes toward math, vegetables, gardening, and new experiences) can create an excellent beginning to a more neutral conversation before applying the same Attitude Exercise to one of the populations addressed in Making Friends (children with disabilities, diverse racial/ethnic backgrounds, diverse family structures, or different languages).

They [individuals with special needs] are like you. —Maria, 7 years old

4. It also is important to remember that even the absence of experiences with specific populations of people can influence attitude development. Because of this, it is recommended that a discussion of this phenomenon be undertaken with a real-life experience. For example, when the Attitude Exercise was piloted with college students who were studying to become teachers, one student talked about never having experiences with African American people. The student went on to explain how this shaped his view of a whole population in a negative way. In the absence of personal experiences, he used the news of arrests and other negative media input to inform his attitudes, and he went on to explain that he now saw how one-dimensional and uninformed those attitudes were in the absence of having direct experiences. This example illustrates that when completing the Attitude Exercise, one can use either direct experiences or the absence of direct experiences.

5. Finally, as a person develops and learns, both negative and positive attitudes are formed. Therefore, it is important when completing the Attitude Exercise to have a balance of examples that reflect both positive and negative attitudes.

To try this exercise, select a childhood experience focusing on an item, situation, or event that provided the early perceptions for a lasting attitude. Complete the Attitude Exercise (Appendix 3.1) to identify the early beginnings of an attitude (ideas, feelings, and actions) that were reinforced by teachers, family members, or other caregivers. Once the Attitude Exercise is completed, members of the Making Friends program (e.g., teachers, paraprofessionals, family members, university students) should discuss their responses to illustrate the three components of an attitude. Then repeat the Attitude Exercise, focusing on one of the populations addressed in this book.

CULTURE AS A CONTEXT FOR ATTITUDE DEVELOPMENT

The next two exercises, titled Remember Who You Are and Unpack Your Perceptions About Diversity, demonstrate how attitude development happens within a larger cultural context that supports positive and negative attitude development through indirect experiences, direct experiences, and the messages given by one's primary social group (the family). But first, let's step back and think about the concepts of culture and cultural competence.

What Is Culture?

Culture refers to a collection of values and beliefs that are held by a specific social group (e.g., a family). Culture is typically reflected by shared language, traditions, and dressing and eating habits, and it is depicted in literature, drama, and other artifacts. In essence, shared practices, beliefs, and values provide a sense of identification and belongingness to the members of a group, which keeps a culture alive.

Culture is multidimensional. It is important to note that a person or family's culture is a collective set of values and beliefs that come from many distinct identities, such as race, ethnicity, religion, socioeconomic status, and so forth (see Figure 3.5). The multidimensional aspects of culture are unique to each person and each family. For example, some families may identify more or less with specific dimensions of their culture. When asked about one's cultural identities, one man said, "I am an early childhood teacher, a Midwesterner, and a black man of German descent who was raised by a Methodist preacher." In this example, occupation, geographic locale, race, gender, ethnicity, and religion were all mentioned, all of which made up this man's cultural identity. With further questioning, he went on to say that the two most influential cultural dimensions from his childhood were his religion and race, tracing his current values and beliefs back to those two dimensions of his family culture, which provided a lens through which he viewed the world as a child.

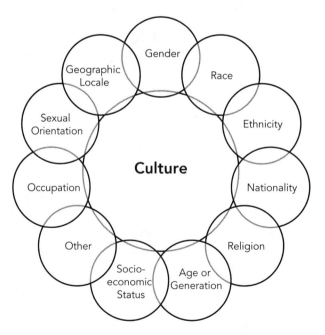

Figure 3.5. Culture.

Like this example, most of us have many identities. One individual may strongly identify with being bilingual and Korean. Someone else may have a strong identity as a Jewish immigrant from Romania. Still another person may identify with being a farmer and a Pacific Islander.

PLEASE   THANK YOU   SORRY

Some cultural identities are well established and constant across the lifespan. Over the course of a lifetime, different cultural identities take a leading role in shaping the way one views the world. Many cultural identities are constant (e.g., race, ethnicity, family history, and background). For example, a teacher might be Chinese American or Native American or a child of Russian immigrants. These longstanding or well-established identities influence values and beliefs, which are passed on from family members. They also influence celebratory customs, child-rearing practices, and everyday interactions. In essence, these identities provide a lens through which to view the world as young children observe and learn actions or behaviors based on the deep-seated values associated with these enduring identities.

Some cultural identities are transitory and change across the lifespan. As a child grows into a young adult, cultural identities can shift, making way for new values and beliefs. For example, as one ages, being a part of the football team or the high school debate team can open one up to new values. Life events also can change cultural identities. For example, one might change religions based on marriage to someone of another faith. Becoming a parent may be a new identity that results in a heightened sense of awareness, thoughts, feelings, and changes in behaviors related to that new identity. A new dad may become a more cautious driver, knowing that there is a baby in the car, or a new mom may have different ideas about mealtimes and foods to ensure that the child has a routine and healthy eating habits. Cultural identities can be associated with personal milestones (e.g., becoming a teenager, a parent, a grandparent, a wife) and professional milestones (e.g., obtaining a new job title or occupation, becoming a college student). All of this is quite natural. Therefore, it is important to recognize that some cultural identities persist across a lifetime while other cultural identities play a prominent yet transitory role across the lifespan.

Culture is dynamic. Whether a cultural identity is constant (e.g., race, ethnicity, family history, background) or variable (e.g., religion, marital status, occupation), culture can be dynamic or subject to change. For example, one's family culture may change because of an increase in a parent's educational level that in turn affects knowledge, beliefs, values, and child-rearing practices. At the same time, because the family member has more education, the family may have more income, which might result in eating out more often, which disrupts the family custom of gathering at mealtime and could change the passing on of values as conversations with family members become more limited. Another example of the dynamic

Yebon remembered friends from her preschool class who were in wheelchairs. She told us why she liked them.
—*Ms. Jung*

nature of culture is the impact of modernization, such as technology. Ubiquitous access to the Internet, cell phones, and television invites many other influences for young children, which can potentially affect the transmission of family values and beliefs and even the way in which family members communicate with one another.

While these changes in culture are the result of a gradual evolution over time (e.g., television, phones, Internet, access to higher education, increased income), some cultural changes occur as a result of new laws. For example, the Education for All Handicapped Children Act (EHA) of 1975, now called IDEA, was a watershed moment that led to cultural, social, and political changes for children with disabilities and their families. Over time, families with children with disabilities brought their children out of institutional or home settings. Because of EHA, family members began to receive social and financial support, many were able to go to work, and they along with their children were no longer excluded from society.

Military conflicts also can lead to cultural change. For example, after the Civil War in the United States, the focus was on freedom and education for former slaves (Williams, 2005). In fact, more than 3,000 schools were established for freed slaves, including many of the first colleges for African Americans (e.g., Fisk, Howard University, Hampton College). Over time, this brought about changes in the independence, education, and socioeconomic status of many, leading to a gradual shift in the families of many African Americans.

What are the implications of culture being dynamic and multidimensional? What does this mean for students in kindergarten through Grade 2? What does this mean for the Making Friends program?

- Because culture is dynamic, any culture (even one of negative attitudes or nonacceptance) is susceptible to change. It implies that attitudes, which develop within a cultural context, can change.

- Because cultures are multidimensional, each individual is influenced by a combination of cultures. For example, a person might be from a high-income family, be Baptist, have Down syndrome, be Caucasian, and live fairly independently with modest supports in a house with two peers. We cannot confine our understanding of others to a single characteristic or stereotype (e.g., all people with disabilities are helpless, all Caucasian people are racist, all people who do not know English are uneducated). And because we know that the culture of a person is multilayered, it can be exciting to get to know others as individuals with many dimensions.

- Finally, both of these realities (the dynamic and multidimensional nature of culture) imply that programs such as Making Friends can make a difference in influencing children's early perceptions and attitudes regarding diversity—that understanding of human differences and similarities can change, as can attitudes. Collectively, these facts highlight the need to understand one's own culture and the cultures of children, especially in today's diverse early childhood settings. In doing so, all of us can become more culturally competent.

He often demonstrated the words he learned to sign.
—Mrs. Davis

What Is Cultural Competence?

To address the needs of children in increasingly diverse classrooms, the National Education Association (n.d.-a) stresses the need for teachers to demonstrate skills in five basic cultural competency areas (adapted from Diller & Moule, 2005):

1. *Valuing diversity.* Educators must accept and respect differences—different cultural backgrounds and customs, different ways of communicating, and different traditions and values.

2. *Being culturally self-aware.* Culture—the sum total of an individual's experiences, knowledge, skills, beliefs, values, and interests—shapes educators' sense of who they are and where they fit within their family, school, community, and society.

3. *Dynamics of difference.* Educators must know what can go wrong in cross-cultural communication and how to respond to these situations.

4. *Knowledge of students' culture.* Educators must have some base knowledge of their students' culture so that student behaviors can be understood in their proper cultural context.

5. *Institutionalizing cultural knowledge and adapting to diversity.* Culturally competent educators, and the institutions in which they work, can take a step further by institutionalizing cultural knowledge so as to adapt to and better serve diverse populations. Institutionalizing cultural knowledge can be undertaken in several ways, such as providing schoolwide training, adopting guidelines, and instituting ongoing year-round programs (e.g., Making Friends) that are focused on increasing cultural awareness and adapting to diversity.

*I learned about special needs.
—Joshua, 5½ years old*

The philosophy of the Making Friends program is consistent with all of these tenets of cultural competence, stressing the imperative to create culturally responsive inclusive early childhood settings for all children. To realize these tenets requires that teachers and school administrators go beyond the notion of dedicating one day for celebrating diversity but rather infuse strategies and celebrations of diversity into everyday, ongoing activities in the school and class setting. The next two tools, the Remember Who You Are exercise and the Unpack Your Perceptions About Diversity exercise, are provided to enable teachers to become more culturally self-aware and better understand how attitudes develop within a cultural context.

THE REMEMBER WHO YOU ARE EXERCISE

The Remember Who You Are exercise focuses on one or two cultural identities that shape a person's values and beliefs over time. This exercise illustrates how cultural identities influence and shape early perceptions, which gradually solidify positive and negative attitude development. Let's look at Figure 3.6, an exercise completed by Hannah, a preservice teacher, during the field-testing of Making Friends.

Remember Who You Are

Identify one or two *cultural identities* that shape who you are (shape the way you think and act). Who or what shaped these strong identities?	I am . . . a strong woman (gender identification).
	   My father fostered this strong gender identity as he helped raise his four sisters and four daughters in a time when women were not seen as equal to men.
		I am . . . a Southerner.
		   This identity began to develop when I was quite young, as I spent most of my formative years in the southern part of the United States. I was profoundly and positively impacted by growing up in the South during the 1960s, in a way that I might not have experienced had I grown up somewhere else.

Name one or two *values or beliefs* that come from or are associated with your identities.	I believe or I value. . . . • I believe women are strong and equal to men. • I believe everyone (boys and girls) should have choices. • I do not believe in gender-specific toys or roles.	I believe or I value. . . . • I believe respect for others and manners are essential skills, because we are interconnected to all others and life is very relational. • I believe it takes enormous courage, humility, and strong relational skills to be different—to be a minority within any group. • I believe we can peacefully live in a diverse society when we respectfully listen to and talk with one another in ways that honor and celebrate our differences.
What were the *indirect experiences* that encouraged you to have these values and attitudes?	I was introduced to stories about strong women like Sojourner Truth and Susan B. Anthony.	I saw the absence of people of color in books and media, and I talked about it with my dad. I watched the news about the riots. I listened to the civil rights leaders and discussed these events with my parents.
What were the *direct experiences* that influenced you?	I was praised for speaking with confidence, making my own clothing, repairing the car, making bread, cooking, and gardening.	My parents brought people from diverse backgrounds into our home and took us to places with people that were different from us with regard to race, ethnicity, and religion. They encouraged conversations about all that was happening around us as we experienced curfews during race riots. I later would go to demonstrations and ride buses with people of color, where I was in the minority.
What was the *overriding message* from your family?	I was told/taught that . . . • I can do anything. • people who do not respect women are narrow-minded.	I was told/taught that . . . • having good manners and understanding and respecting others were critical skills during the Civil Rights movement. • that I could be a part of the solution or a part of the problem. • to not speak up (respectfully disagree) or to not challenge injustice was to be a part of the problem.
How are *your behaviors still influenced* by your values?	I usually . . . • avoid people who do not recognize the equality of women or equality of all people. • have little sympathy for "hand wringing" or whining. • read about strong women from other cultures.	I usually . . . • am respectful and courteous in my interactions. • place my own children in the midst of diverse populations and discuss the historical and current realities of minorities. • read about other cultures so as to better understand other people and their perspectives. • relish work in other cultures and countries because I see we have a great deal to learn from one another.
How are your *expectations of others* influenced by your values and beliefs?	I expect others to . . . • treat all as equal.	I expect others to . . . • to be respectful and courteous. • to be part of the solution. • to understand how their culture influences them.

Figure 3.6.   Remember Who You Are exercise completed by Hannah.

What Can Be Learned from the Remember Who You Are Exercise?

- *How were the identities of Hannah shaped by her early childhood experiences?* Hannah's family members were very focused on making sure their beliefs about the equality of all people (regardless of gender or race) were passed on through the conversations and the actions they modeled.

- *What were examples of direct experiences, indirect experiences, and the primary social group that shaped Hannah's attitude formation?* The direct experiences included her family members bringing diverse people into their home and also teaching her skills that shaped her confidence and her attitudes (e.g., about speaking up in respectful ways, problem solving, repairing the car). The indirect experiences included passing on the oral histories of strong women of both races (African American and Caucasian), reading books, watching television, and having discussions with her father. The messages from her family (her primary social group) included positive attitudes about racial diversity and equality of women. Her parents praised Hannah when she exhibited respectful conversations and actions; they consistently focused on Hannah strengthening her abilities and boosting her self-confidence.

Students are talking about seeing people in the community who have disabilities.
—Mr. McDonnell

- *How were the messages of the broader culture and era in which Hannah grew up alike or different from the messages given by her family? Were any new insights gained from reading about the respondent's experience?* It is clear that the broader culture did not share the same values and beliefs as Hannah's family. It seems that because of this, Hannah's family members had to be very vigilant about sending a different message than the one held by the broader culture. It is remarkable that Hannah said that she was positively influenced growing up in the South during a pretty difficult time period. One insight gained was this: though a situation can be very negative, the experience can still have a positive outcome. That was really encouraging.

Now, read through more responses to the Remember Who You Are exercise (Table 3.1) to see how the cultural identities of others influenced their development.

Use the same prompts from earlier to reflect on what can be learned from these responses.

Now it is time to try out this exercise. Complete the Remember Who You Are exercise (Appendix 3.2) and have a discussion with others who are participating in your Making Friends program (e.g., teachers, paraprofessionals, adult volunteers) to identify specific ways in which one's cultural identities provide messages about diversity through indirect

Table 3.1. Sample responses to Remember Who You Are exercise

What are your *cultural identities*?	<ul><li>I am an Asian woman from California and from a military family.</li><li>I grew up poor on the south side of Chicago. I am black; my family is Muslim, and we immigrated to the United States from Kenya.</li><li>I am a gay African American woman from Georgia and the daughter of a preacher.</li><li>I am a middle-class Jewish woman of German descent from New York.</li><li>I am from a biracial family who lived on a farm in the Midwestern part of the United States.</li></ul>
What *values* do you hold that reflect one or two of your cultural identities? What are the beliefs that you had as a child?	<ul><li>During my childhood, I believed that anyone who was from another religious faith was a bad person.</li><li>I believed people who were not like me were low class. I had such a strong identity to my own culture that I looked down on those who were different (e.g., African American, gay, middle class).</li><li>I still believe self-sufficiency is the ideal. I do not believe in living off of government. I grew up proud and very independent because we lived off the land as farmers. I almost resented anyone who did not grow his or her own food. As a child, I believed they were lazy and they could not appreciate how hard it was to be a farmer.</li></ul>
How were those values transmitted to you? What were your *indirect and direct experiences and the messages from your family*?	<ul><li>My parents made negative remarks about those who were black. I grew up doing the same until I was 30 and had a colleague who was black, who later became a close friend.</li><li>We never watched movies or television shows unless there was a Christian message. My dad always checked to see what movies were on the approved Christian list. As a result, for years, I thought any other religion was evil, and I grew up suspicious of others who were not of the same faith.</li><li>Every time we were in stores in poor neighborhoods, my mom insisted that we wash our hands when we got home. She never did that when we went to stores in middle-class or wealthy neighborhoods. As a child, I thought all poor people were dirty.</li><li>When I saw a person with a disability, I would point at them. My mom said to stop pointing and talking about them. So we never discussed it, and I grew up thinking they were scary.</li></ul>
What *behaviors do you exhibit* that reflect your values?	<ul><li>I avoided all minority groups. Without even thinking about it, I passed this same message on to my children. That was the easiest thing to do.</li><li>I still get nervous when I go into poor neighborhoods.</li><li>I would make fun of people with disabilities throughout my high school years. It is embarrassing to admit that.</li><li>My whole perspective about people with disabilities changed when my sister had a child with a disability. She talked about how hard it was for my niece to make friends. Now, I teach my children to be friends with their cousin and others with disabilities at their school.</li></ul>
What *behaviors do you expect of others* that reflect your values?	<ul><li>I expect Asian people to live near each other, stick together, and sit together on the bus.</li><li>I expect others to stay in their own neighborhoods. I get worried when I see someone like them walking in my neighborhood.</li><li>I expect everyone to be treated with respect.</li></ul>
What happens when there is a disconnect between your expectations and the behavior of others? How do you resolve this disconnect?	<ul><li>There are misunderstandings. We need to start talking about it, but I don't know how.</li><li>Feelings get hurt and nobody talks about it. But that does not help.</li><li>It is awkward and uncomfortable, and it needs to be addressed.</li></ul>
What could you do to promote greater understanding and respect for diversity?	<ul><li>I took my own children to different houses of worship so we could learn about other people's beliefs.</li><li>I found pen pals for my students. Their pen pals are from other parts of the United States, so they could learn to appreciate the diversity around us.</li><li>I introduced myself to teachers at my school that I had never talked to before. I asked them if we could have lunch meetings to get to know one another and to help break down barriers.</li></ul>

experiences, direct experiences, and the conversations and actions of one's first social group, the family. Then continue to the next section to delve deeper into understanding how attitudes are developed and shaped.

THE UNPACK YOUR PERCEPTIONS ABOUT DIVERSITY EXERCISE

So far, the Attitude Exercise demonstrated that attitudes are multicomponent constructs that include ideas, feelings, and behaviors. The Remember Who You Are exercise demonstrated that the three primary influences on attitude development (indirect experiences, direct experiences, and the primary social group) affect a person within the context of one's longstanding culture identities.

Students are talking more about disabilities and using sign language.
—Ms. Simons

Now it is time to apply what was learned from these two exercises to the next exercise, Unpack Your Perceptions About Diversity. This exercise is intended to extend the Attitude Exercise by applying the same three components of an attitude to one's early experiences with people who have a disability, represent a different race or ethnicity, speak another language, or are from a family structure that is different from one's own (e.g., foster or adoptive family, same-sex parents, single parent, raised by a grandparent).

Unpack Your Perceptions About Diversity focuses on how early perceptions of people develop and shape one's attitudes by addressing the following questions:

- What are your earliest experiences/memories of someone who was different from you (with regard to ability, race/ethnicity, language, or family structure)? Describe an early memory from your home, neighborhood, community, or school.

- What were the messages about diversity from your family? What were your indirect and direct experiences? Were they positive or negative, accepting or rejecting?

- Who gave the messages and how? How did your family members and teachers reinforce positive or negative attitudes?

- How did those messages affect your early perceptions of individuals who were different from you? How did you think, feel, and act?

- Do you still have those same ideas and feelings or engage in those same behaviors?

  - If yes, how have your original perceptions been reinforced?

  - If no, what happened to change them?

See Figures 3.7–3.10 for examples from four people who responded to Unpack Your Perceptions About Diversity. Think about the similarities and differences across the examples.

Unpack Your Perceptions About Diversity: Jamal

Describe your early perceptions about diversity in terms of one of the following: disabilities, race/ethnicity, language, or family structure.

1. What are your earliest experiences/memories of someone with this difference?

   I remember seeing a crippled man who walked in our neighborhood.

2. Were the experiences positive or negative? What were the messages given to you about someone who has this difference?

   Thinking back on it, I think the message was negative.

3. Who gave you these messages and how were the messages delivered?

   My mom; when I asked her about the man, she said not to point or talk about him and to stay away from him.

4. How did those messages affect your early perceptions of individuals who were different from you? How did you think, feel, and act?

   I thought he was a bad person. The conversation made me afraid of him. I would cross the street if I saw him coming near me.

5. Do you still have those same ideas and feelings or engage in those same behaviors? If yes, how have your original perceptions been reinforced? If no, what happened to change them?

   Yes. Over time, I saw others laugh at him and at other people with disabilities. I saw many people with disabilities begging for money in the street. I came to think of them as dirty. And most kids with disabilities were not in my classes, so we never really had contact with them. To this day, I am uncomfortable around people with disabilities, and even though I know better, my feelings of discomfort persist. I think talking about it would have helped, but that did not happen back then. I think not talking about it and keeping people separated in school reinforced my ideas, feelings, and behavior.

Figure 3.7. Jamal's early perceptions about people with disabilities.

Unpack Your Perceptions About Diversity: Sandra

Describe your early perceptions about diversity in terms of one of the following: disabilities, (race/ethnicity,) language, or family structure.

1. What are your earliest experiences/memories of someone with this difference?

   I am a black woman, and my earliest memories of contact with white people started when I was about 3 or 4 years old. Sometimes I went to work with my daddy, who worked down at the fishing docks. I met some white men who worked with him.

2. Were the experiences positive or negative? What were the messages given to you about someone who has this difference?

   The experiences and messages were positive. Everyone was friendly, and they played games with me when I was at the docks. Also, some of them came over to our house for fried catfish dinners.

3. Who gave you these messages and how were the messages delivered?

   My dad. I used to ask him all kinds of questions like, "When is my skin going to get white like Mr. Jones?" He always laughed and said, "Mr. Jones does have some beautiful skin, but your skin is also beautiful. And most of us keep the skin we were born with." His answers were usually matter-of-fact and positive.

4. How did those messages affect your early perceptions of individuals who were different from you? How did you think, feel, and act?

   I liked my dad's friends. They were all friendly. I really was shocked when I got older and realized that many people of different races did not like each other. I was proud of my dad, who accepted people for who they were.

5. Do you still have those same ideas and feelings or engage in those same behaviors? If yes, how have your original perceptions been reinforced? If no, what happened to change them?

   Absolutely. In high school, I joined clubs that focused on antibullying, and I dated people of different races.

Figure 3.8.   Sandra's early perceptions about racial differences.

Unpack Your Perceptions About Diversity: Anshula

Describe your early perceptions about diversity in terms of one of the following: disabilities, race/ethnicity, (language,) or family structure.

1. What are your earliest experiences/memories of someone with this difference?

    Every Sunday, we went downtown to buy hot tamales from Señor Martinez, who had a little stand under an oak tree. He had the whitest teeth, and he smiled real big each time he saw us. We saw him so often that he began teaching Spanish words and phrases to me and my siblings.

2. Were the experiences positive or negative? What were the messages given to you about someone who has this difference?

    Both the experiences and messages were positive. My parents would rehearse new Spanish words with us before we arrived to pick up our hot tamales, and we would practice at dinner, too. "Me gustan los tamales. ¿Te gustan los tamales?"

3. Who gave you these messages and how were the messages delivered?

    Both of my parents learned to say simple phrases with us. Our family later traveled to Mexico. To prepare for the trip, we went to Mexican restaurants so we could order food in Spanish.

4. How did those messages affect your early perceptions of individuals who were different from you? How did you think, feel, and act?

    Meeting people who spoke other languages and then learning from them made me feel proud and boosted my own confidence. I thought it was cool! I also remember thinking that people who speak more than one language must be pretty smart.

5. Do you still have those same ideas and feelings or engage in those same behaviors? If yes, how have your original perceptions been reinforced? If no, what happened to change them?

    Yes! I went on to study Spanish and work in countries where Spanish was spoken. I later studied sign language and became a speech therapist. I think my career path was influenced by these early experiences.

Figure 3.9.   Anshula's early perceptions about language differences.

Unpack Your Perceptions About Diversity: Mike

Describe your early perceptions about diversity in terms of one of the following: disabilities, race/ethnicity, language, or family structure.

1. What are your earliest experiences/memories of someone with this difference?

   I was 5 years old when I met a boy who lived with his grandmother. He did not have parents.

2. Were the experiences positive or negative? What were the messages given to you about someone who has this difference?

   I think the experience was negative. When I asked about it, my mom said that his parents could not take care of him. So I thought there was something wrong with him or his parents.

3. Who gave you these messages and how were the messages delivered?

   My mom. After she told us that his parents could not take care of him, my mom said we should not talk about him anymore. That made me think there was something bad happening at their house.

4. How did those messages affect your early perceptions of individuals who were different from you? How did you think, feel, and act?

   I was creeped out; I actually thought there was something scary about the boy, the grandmother, and the house. I never played with him. I used to think that anyone who did not have a mom and a dad must have something wrong with them.

5. Do you still have those same ideas and feelings or engage in those same behaviors? If yes, how have your original perceptions been reinforced? If no, what happened to change them?

   No, my ideas about children who come from all kinds of home situations changed when I was in college. I met all kinds of people who were raised by one or two parents, foster and adoptive parents, or two dads. I think I was open to change because my college roommate became my best friend. He was a foster kid with two dads. He talked about how hard it was to be a foster kid and how thrilled he was to have a family. Of course, now I realize that the world needs all kinds of families.

Figure 3.10.   Mike's early perceptions about unique family structures.

What Can Be Learned from Unpack Your Perceptions About Diversity?

What similarities exist across all these early childhood experiences?

- By naming the similarities that were previously identified from the Attitude Exercise, one should be able to explain the components of an attitude (ideas, feelings, and behaviors).

- By naming the similarities that were previously identified from the Remember Who You Are exercise, one should be able to explain how attitudes develop from early perceptions, which are reinforced within a culture (through indirect experiences, direct experiences, and the primary social group).

Now it is time to think about perceptions that exist about the diversity areas focused on in the Making Friends program. Complete the Unpack Your Perceptions About Diversity exercise (Appendix 3.3) to understand how your perceptions about diversity were formed. Select a particular diversity area (disability, race/ethnicity, language, or family structure) and remember to focus on early childhood experiences.

After completing this exercise, either discuss what you discovered with others (e.g., colleagues, coteacher, assistants) or self-check your responses to these questions, referring to Figure 2.3.

*Another thing I liked about the project was sending the books home, and I had a lot of parents comment about the books, and it showed that a lot was going on.
—Mr. Van Hoorn*

- Are you able to identify the components of an attitude from your responses?

- Are you able to describe the background information on how your attitudes were influenced?

If the answer to both of these questions is "yes," then you have a good understanding of the basics of attitude formation and you are off to a good start in creating your own Making Friends program!

The next section of this chapter focuses on another useful tool, the Diversity in School Environments exercise, which can be used to examine the diversity represented in a classroom and school environment.

THE DIVERSITY IN SCHOOL ENVIRONMENTS EXERCISE

According to the National Education Association (n.d.-b), diversity in school environments can be defined as

> the sum of the ways that people are both alike and different. The dimensions of diversity include race, ethnicity, gender, sexual orientation, language, culture, religion, mental and physical ability, class, and immigration status. Moreover, addressing diversity in class settings encompasses opportunities to learn about and experience languages and cultures through classroom curriculum, print and visual media and conversation with peers, all of which enriches and prepares each of us for life in global society.

However, the representation of diversity in school environments (e.g., print and visual media, curricula) has its challenges.

It was not so long ago that people with disabilities and people from diverse minority groups were absent from many books, curricula, and media, and when they did begin to appear in visual and print media, they were often presented in a negative light (Barnes, 1992; Johnson & Lewis, 1998; Pescosolido, Grauerholz, & Milkie, 1997). In fact, Clark (1969, 1972) identified four stages of media representation to illustrate the depiction of minorities: nonrepresentation (exclusion), ridicule (objects of humor or pity, subservient), regulation (limited, socially acceptable role), and respect (fully developed characters with positive and negative attributes). Because representation in print and visual media can affect the development of one's self-concept and sense of belonging, as well as perceptions of and attitudes toward others (Rivadeneyra, Ward, & Gordon, 2007; Roethler, 1998), it is critical that the materials in early childhood environments reflect the diversity in the classroom and community and are thoughtfully selected with regard to the messages they send to children.

For example, as the Making Friends program was being field-tested, one teacher who had taught for 3 years described her experience with a child with a disability, who, like children from various races and ethnicities, was often underrepresented in classroom curricula and print and visual media:

> After talking about animals that live in different habitats, we began reading books about children who lived in different settings. Some of the books were about children who lived in an apartment in the city. Some books were about children who lived on farms or in houses on the outskirts of towns. At the end of the unit, when asking my students what they noticed about the children in the books, one child spoke up quietly and said, "There are no kids like me—kids with disabilities. Where do kids like me live?"

*Students are talking with their peers more often.
—Ms. Cola*

The teacher went on to explain that this was one of those unforgettable moments, for as she looked around her classroom and thought about her curriculum, she realized that the child was right—children with disabilities are often not represented in the world around them. The only image of a child with a disability was the one posted once a year for the March of Dimes fundraiser. While such efforts can be beneficial, what message might this send to that child and others? If the only classroom image a child with a disability sees is this poster, *possible* messages it could send are that children with disabilities are in need of a handout, dependent on others, and/or not a part of the fabric of the classroom (because the image only appears once a year).

This question, posed by her student, was a turning point for the teacher. She set out to change any unintentional messages of exclusion, dependence, and neediness by the absence of diversity representation in the materials in her classroom. She examined her classroom to ensure that messages of belonging and traits of independence, leadership, equality, respect, and friendship were being portrayed every day. And she looked at other areas of diversity to ensure that all the children in her class were consistently and positively represented in

Diversity in School Environments (DSE)

Teacher: <u>Miss Londie</u>   Date: <u>7/29/15</u>

Directions

- The DSE contains questions that enable teachers to describe the materials in their classroom and their school that depict individuals from diverse backgrounds (e.g., ability, race and ethnicity, language, and family structure). There are no right or wrong answers to the items on the DSE; the tool is simply meant to help you identify how individuals from diverse backgrounds are represented in your classroom and school.

- The DSE will take approximately 20 minutes to complete. It is divided into six sections:

  1. Classroom Environment: Visual and Aesthetic Elements
  2. Curriculum
  3. Books
  4. Dramatic Play
  5. Language
  6. Schoolwide Environment

- After completing the DSE, you may want to discuss your results with another teacher or an administrator who is familiar with your classroom setting. A trusted colleague may notice additional ways that you have represented diversity and may have suggestions for ways that you can increase representations of diversity.

- It will be helpful for you to revisit and rescore this tool periodically to reflect changes in your classroom and school environments.

How to Complete and Score the DSE

- Respond with "yes" or "no" to the questions about each aspect of diversity represented in your classroom.

- For each item that you answer "yes" to, consider adding examples to describe the material or activity that fulfills the requirement named in the item, as in this example:

	Y/N	Example
1. Are there images of children with disabilities in your room (e.g., photos or pictures reflecting people with differing abilities)?	Y	Poster of children with diverse abilities reading together—displayed in book center.

- All "yes" responses receive 1 point. All "no" responses receive 0 points. Further information about scoring is provided at the end of the DSE.

Section 1—Classroom Environment: Visual and Aesthetic Elements

Section 1A. Diversity in Your Classroom: *Disability*	Y/N	Example

1. Are there images of children with disabilities (e.g., photos or pictures reflecting people with differing abilities)?
  • If "NO," skip the remaining questions in Section 1A.
  • If "YES," complete Section 1A.
	Y	Posters of child in a wheelchair

2. Do these images reflect current life (are the photos or pictures up-to-date)?	N	
3. Indicate if these images have an adequate balance.		
a. Is there more than one person with a disability?	N	
b. Is there more than one type of disability represented?	N	

Figure 3.11. Diversity in School Environments exercise completed by Miss Londie, kindergarten teacher.

4. Do these images show differently abled people . . .		
a. of various ethnic backgrounds?	N	
b. of various ages (adults and children)?	N	
c. doing work?	Y	Doctor's office
d. engaging in recreational activities?	Y	
e. with family members?	N	
f. in a positive way (active, independent)?	Y	Dolls using wheelchair
Subtotal: Add the number of YES responses for Section 1A	4	

Section 1B: Diversity in Your Classroom: *Race and Ethnicity*	Y/N	Example
1. Are there images of children of different races/ethnicities (e.g., photos or pictures reflecting people of different races)? • If "NO," skip the remaining questions in Section 1B. • If "YES," complete Section 1B.	Y	
2. Do these images reflect current life (are the photos or pictures up-to-date)?	Y	
3. Indicate if these images have an adequate balance.		
a. Is there more than one person from a diverse race or ethnicity?	Y	
b. Are there multiple races and ethnicities represented?	Y	
4. Do these images show people from diverse racial and ethnic backgrounds . . .		
a. with a variety of abilities?	Y	
b. of various ages (adults and children)?	Y	
c. doing work?	Y	
d. engaging in recreational activities?	Y	
e. with family members?	Y	
f. in a positive way (active, independent)?	Y	
Subtotal: Add the number of YES responses for Section 1B	10	

Section 1C: Diversity in Your Classroom: *Family Structure*	Y/N	Example
1. Are there images of children from a variety of family structures (e.g., photos or pictures reflecting different family structures)? • If "NO," skip the remaining questions in Section 1C. • If "YES," complete Section 1C.	Y	Photos of adopted children with their families
2. Do these images reflect current life (are the photos or pictures up-to-date)?	Y	Personal photos
3. Indicate if these images have an adequate balance.		
a. Is there more than one person from a diverse family structure?	N	
b. Are there multiple family structures represented?	N	
4. Do these images show people from diverse family structures . . .		
a. with a variety of abilities?	N	

(continued)

Figure 3.11. (*continued*)

	Y/N	Example
b. of various ages (adults and children)?	N	
c. doing work?	Y	
d. engaging in recreational activities?	Y	
e. in a positive way (active, independent)?	Y	
Subtotal: Add the number of YES responses for Section 1C	**5**	

Section 1D: Diversity in Your Classroom: *Language*	Y/N	Example
1. Are there images of children who use a variety of languages (e.g., photos or pictures reflecting different languages)? • If "NO," skip the remaining questions in Section 1D. • If "YES," complete Section 1D.	N	
2. Do these images reflect current life (are the photos or pictures up-to-date)?	N	
3. Indicate if these images have an adequate balance.		
a. Is there more than one person who uses a different language?	N	
b. Are there multiple languages represented (e.g., Spanish, sign language)?	N	
4. Do these images show people who use a different language or way of communicating . . .		
a. with a variety of abilities?	N	
b. of various ages (adults and children)?	N	
c. doing work?	N	
d. engaging in recreational activities?	N	
e. with family members?	N	
f. in a positive way (active, independent)?	N	
Subtotal: Add the number of YES responses for Section 1D	**0**	

Section 2—Curriculum

Diversity: *disability, race/ethnicity, language, family structure*	Y/N	Example
1. When images of people in different occupations are presented in your curriculum, are differently abled people represented?	N	
2. When images of important and/or famous individuals, past and present, are presented in your class curriculum, are differently abled people represented? If yes, who? Answer YES if more than two are named. Examples include Franklin Delano Roosevelt (polio), Helen Keller (visual and hearing impairment), Magic Johnson and Robin Williams (ADHD), Whoopi Goldberg and Tom Cruise (learning disability), and Stephen Hawking (ALS / Lou Gehrig's disease).	Y	Runner who had polio as a child
3. When images of people in different occupations are presented in your curriculum, are people from different races and ethnicities represented?	Y	Community helpers unit

4. When images of important and/or famous individuals, past and present, are presented in your class curriculum, are different races and ethnicities represented? If yes, who? Answer YES if more than two are named. Examples include Barack Obama and Martin Luther King Jr. (African American), Cesar Chavez (Latino), Casimir Polaski (Polish), Yo-Yo Ma (Chinese), Squanto (Native American), and Apolo Anton Ohno (Japanese American).	Y	Mostly individuals who are black or white
5. When images of people in different occupations are presented in your curriculum, are people who speak different languages represented?	Y	Spanish speaking English speaking
6. When images of important and/or famous individuals, past and present, are presented in your class curriculum, are people who speak different languages represented? If yes, who? Answer YES if more than two are named. Examples include Marlee Matlin and Heather Whitestone (American Sign Language), Jodie Foster (English, French, German, Spanish, Italian), Sammy Sosa (Spanish), Mila Kunis (English, Russian), Kobe Bryant (English, Italian), and Johnny Depp (English, French).	Y	But not the focus
7. When images of people in different occupations are presented in your curriculum, are different family structures represented?	Y	Single parents
8. When images of important and/or famous individuals, past and present, are presented in your class curriculum, are people from different family structures represented? If yes, who? Answer YES if more than two are named. Examples include Toni Morrison, Coretta Scott King, and Jamie Foxx (single parent); Angelina Jolie, Dave Thomas, and Raven-Symoné (adoptive parents); and Neil Patrick Harris, Ellen DeGeneres, Rosie O'Donnell, and Guillermo Diaz (LGBT).	N	
Subtotal: Add the number of YES responses for Section 2	6	

Section 3—Books

Diversity: *disability, race/ethnicity, language, family structure*	Y/N	Example
1. Do children have access to books in your classroom that reflect children/adults with diverse abilities?	Y	
2. Do children have access to books in your classroom that reflect children/adults from diverse racial and ethnic backgrounds?	Y	But only during Black History Month
3. Do children have access to books in your classroom that reflect children/adults who use different languages? Answer YES if more than two languages are featured. Examples include sign language, braille, augmentative/alternative communication (AAC), and spoken/written languages other than English (e.g., French, Spanish, Vietnamese).	N	
4. Do children have access to books in your classroom that reflect diverse family structures? Answer YES if more than two family structures are featured. Examples include single-parent families, adoptive families, foster families, families with incarcerated family members, and families with two moms or two dads.	N	
Subtotal: Add the number of YES responses for Section 3	2	

(continued)

Figure 3.11. *(continued)*

Section 4—Dramatic Play

Diversity: *disability, race/ethnicity, language, family structure*	Y/N	Example
1. Do children have access to tools/materials used by people with diverse abilities (e.g., crutches, braces, wheelchairs, walkers, canes, magnifying glasses, eyeglasses)?	Y	In dramatic play
2. Do any dolls (bought or homemade) have different kinds of abilities?	Y	In dramatic play
3. Do children have access to tools/materials used by people from various racial or ethnic backgrounds (e.g., food, cooking utensils, clothing or toys from different cultures)?	N	
4. Do any dolls (bought or homemade) represent different racial or ethnic backgrounds?	Y	Dolls from different backgrounds
5. Do children have access to tools/materials used by people who speak different languages or communicate in unique ways (e.g., toys and tools that "talk" in other languages, AAC devices, TTYs, braille typewriters, menus in a variety of languages)?	N	
6. Do any dolls (bought or homemade) represent different family structures (e.g., doll families with two moms or two dads, with grandparents as parents, with a single parent, or with biracial parents)?	N	
7. Do dolls (bought or homemade) reflect both genders?	N	
Subtotal: Add the number of YES responses for Section 4	3	

Section 5—Language

Diversity: *language, disability*	Y/N	Example
1. Do children have opportunities in your curriculum to see or use sign language, the Picture Exchange Communication System (PECS), and/or braille (e.g., labeling on furniture and materials, alphabet/number posters, songs, finger games)?	N	
2. Do children have opportunities in your curriculum to see or use spoken/written languages other than English (e.g., labeling on furniture and materials, alphabet/number posters, songs, finger games)?	N	
Subtotal: Add the number of YES responses for Section 5	0	

Section 6—Schoolwide Environment

Diversity: *disability, race/ethnicity, language, family structure*	Y/N	Example
1. Is there a schoolwide program that promotes and encourages interactions between children with and without disabilities?	N	
2. Is there a schoolwide unit/curriculum that provides information about children with disabilities?	N	
3. Are there schoolwide opportunities for children to see or use sign language, PECS, and/or braille (e.g., room or doorway labels)?	Y	Doorways/bathroom
4. Is there a schoolwide program that promotes and encourages interactions between children from diverse racial and ethnic backgrounds?	Y	Different presenters

5. Is there a schoolwide unit/curriculum that provides information about children from diverse racial and ethnic backgrounds?	Y	Photos used with reading
6. Are there schoolwide opportunities for children to see or use materials that represent diverse racial and ethnic backgrounds (e.g., culture fairs or assemblies, flags representing students' countries of origin)?	Y	Multicultural assemblies
7. Is there a schoolwide program that promotes and encourages interactions between children who speak different languages?	N	
8. Is there a schoolwide unit/curriculum that provides information about children who speak/write languages other than English?	N	
9. Are there schoolwide opportunities for children to see or use materials that represent written/spoken languages other than English (e.g., sing-along events including songs in other languages, exit signs, room labels)?	N	
10. Is there a schoolwide program that promotes and encourages interactions between children from different family structures?	N	
11. Is there a schoolwide unit/curriculum that provides information about children from a variety of family structures?	N	
12. Are there schoolwide opportunities for children to see or use materials that represent diverse family structures (e.g., access to LGBT books in the school library, opportunities to invite family members to school)?	N	
Subtotal: Add the number of YES responses for Section 6	4	

Section	Possible points	Points you earned
Classroom Environment: Visual and Aesthetic Elements		
Section 1A: Disability	10	4
Section 1B: Race and Ethnicity	10	10
Section 1C: Family Structure	9	5
Section 1D: Language	10	0
Curriculum		
Section 2	8	6
Books		
Section 3	4	2
Dramatic Play		
Section 4	7	3
Language		
Section 5	2	0
Schoolwide Environment		
Section 6	12	4
Total	**72**	34

Record your points for each section and then the total.

(continued)

Figure 3.11. *(continued)*

What does your total score indicate about the diversity in your classroom and school?

0   My classroom and school have *no representation* of diversity.

1–25   My classroom or school has *low representation* of diversity.

26–47   My classroom and school have *moderate representation of diversity.*

48–72   My classroom and school have *high representation* of diversity.

Concluding Thoughts

Congratulations on completing the DSE! Regardless of your score, you are doing something very valuable for your students by evaluating the ways you represent diversity in your classroom and school. Everyone has to start somewhere, and there is always room for improvement!

Now consider what your next steps will be to better represent diversity in your setting. Use your subtotal scores to identify areas where your classroom or school environment could be improved. Think about materials that you could add to your classroom or school environment, and use the resources found in Chapter 5 to locate materials needed.

Remember to revisit and rescore this tool periodically as you consider possible changes in your school and classroom environments.

Additional Comments and Ideas

Use this space to write down comments or ideas you have (e.g., ideas to share with colleagues, ideas of new ways to represent diversity in your classroom or school).

Londie, Kindergarten

- The score for the materials in my class was 30/60 points, or 50%. The score for materials in my school was 4/12 points, or 33%. My total score was 34/72 points, or 47%. I have room for improvement!

- I could make more materials for the classroom to promote diversity, and I need to look for teachable moments to expand upon the curriculum.

- In the lobby of our school, the pictures only reflect children who are white, until you turn the corner and then you see children of other races and ethnicities. This distribution of pictures needs to be changed. If you do not go down the hallways, you won't see the diversity in the photos.

- My lowest score is in language diversity. I need to find ways to introduce other languages. It is especially important since I have children who speak different languages at home. Also, I did not think of sign language as a different language or the use of the Picture Exchange Communication System (PECS), which is used by some children in our school. That would be great to add.

the world around them. She infused her classroom with visual images, books, toys, and curriculum materials that depicted children with disabilities, children from diverse backgrounds, and children who used other languages.

Unfortunately, this teacher's experience is not unusual. Using the Individuals with Disability Representation tool (Favazza & Odom, 1997), researchers found that the majority of early childhood classrooms do not have adequate materials that depict children with disabilities (Favazza, LaRoe, Phillipsen, & Kumar, 2000). Moreover, even though the field-testing of Making Friends occurred 10 years later in inclusive classes, the same results were found (Ostrosky & Favazza, 2008–2012).

To assist teachers in examining diversity in their classrooms, the Diversity in School Environments (DSE) tool was developed based on Individuals with Disability Representation (Favazza & Odom, 1997). The DSE enables school professionals to observe how children with disabilities, children from diverse family structures, children who use other languages, and children from diverse racial and ethnic backgrounds are represented in classroom and school environments. A completed DSE (Figure 3.11) is provided to illustrate the ways in which one teacher rated the diversity reflected in her classroom. It should be obvious that her classroom and school setting addressed some areas of diversity such as race and ethnicity but did not address other areas. Now it is time to use the DSE (Appendix 3.4) to evaluate the ways in which diversity is represented in your classroom and school. Then use the list of resources provided in Chapter 5 to identify materials that can improve the representation of diversity in your classroom.

In the next section of this chapter, Making Friends Vignettes are provided as examples of conversations about diversity. The purpose of the vignettes is to provide teachers with an opportunity to plan ahead for responses they might provide to children during daily, naturally occurring conversations to promote greater understanding and acceptance of differences.

MAKING FRIENDS VIGNETTES: STRATEGIES FOR INCREASING UNDERSTANDING OF DIVERSITY

In early childhood classrooms, teachers set the general tone of the classroom by modeling kindness, respect, and acceptance of all children and by providing descriptive feedback or praise to students who do the same. While children are learning academic skills, they also are developing social emotional skills. It is important to consider what happens when a teacher observes or overhears conversations that do not reflect kindness and respect or sees that a child does not demonstrate understanding or acceptance of others.

Because students may have questions and encounter challenges related to diversity during everyday events at school, it is important that teachers plan ahead. Completing the self-reflection exercises in this book and evaluating one's classroom are good first steps. But it also is important that teachers are observant of small moments when diversity needs to be addressed and think about how to respond and take advantage of teachable moments when questions arise or when they see things that run counter to what they are teaching their students.

The Making Friends vignettes can be used to help teachers "think on their feet" while addressing everyday challenges and questions related to diversity and differences. Four vignettes are provided to highlight positive and natural responses that teachers can use to increase understanding of differences during everyday school routines. Each vignette focuses on a different type of diversity: disability, language, race/ethnicity, and family structure. Prior to beginning the Making Friends program, all adults who will be a part of the program should read through each vignette and use the prompts provided to think about the best way to respond to the situation. Assume that the situation has occurred in your own classroom, and as a team, discuss possible ways to respond to children. The following are examples of standard responses:

- *Provide a simple explanation* by answering questions in honest, age-appropriate, matter-of-fact ways. In doing so, it encourages children's natural curiosity and conversations about the world around them.

- *Highlight similarities* by asking children to identify ways in which we are all more alike than different. Encouraging a discussion about how we all have similar experiences, feelings, and ideas or how we engage in similar actions will promote increased knowledge and understanding, positive feelings, and respectful behavior. Also, in doing so, adults can model the three components of an attitude (ideas, feelings, and behaviors).

- *Provide positive feedback* by praising children for having caring and respectful conversations. These also can be moments to address specific challenges identified by children in a positive way, thereby facilitating future positive social interactions.

Vignette 1: Conversations and Actions About Children with Disabilities

Ian (age 6, Caucasian) has autism. He lives with his parents and one younger sister. He is really good at reading and math, but he has significant delays in social and communication skills. Ian usually plays alone, rarely engages in social conversations, and has anxiety when encountering unexpected routines. For example, at the beginning of the year, the school needed time to finalize bus routes, so a few school bus numbers and drivers changed. Ian's first-grade teacher carefully explained to Ian that he needed to take a different bus and then walked with him to the school bus. However, when they arrived at the door of the bus, Ian refused to get on the bus. The driver and teacher explained to Ian what happened, but it took more than 10 minutes for him to get on the bus. Other students complained and made comments such as, "Look at him! Why is he standing there? He is so weird."

Questions to Explore Understanding of Children with Disabilities

Provide Simple Explanation: Some people with disabilities may walk, talk, listen, think, or behave differently, but we have many similar feelings and share many things in common.

Highlight Similarities: Has there been a time when you experienced a change that really bothered you? Can you think of a time when something did not go as you had planned and it worried you?

Feelings: How do you feel when you have to do something you don't want to do?

Ideas: Why do you think Ian doesn't want to board the school bus?

Actions: I wonder why Ian didn't just get on the bus. Ian knows you well because you're his classmate. Maybe if Ian sees that you're on the same bus, he won't be upset. You could offer Ian a seat next to you. You could walk onto the bus together as partners.

Provide Positive Feedback: You did a nice job putting yourself in Ian's shoes to think about how he felt and consider why he may have reacted that way to something new and unexpected. By thinking about times when you also felt worried or confused about changes like the bus number or driver, we can see that we're really similar, aren't we?

Vignette 2: Conversations and Actions About Children Who Speak Different Languages

Jisoo (age 5, Korean American) attends kindergarten 5 days a week from 8:00 a.m. to 3:00 p.m. He lives with his parents, who speak both English and Korean, and his grandmother, who only speaks Korean. Before attending kindergarten, Jisoo was cared for at home by his grandmother. His kindergarten teacher, Ms. Reeds, asked Jisoo's parents to write down some words in Korean that could be helpful when communicating with him (e.g., give me [*joo-sae-yo*], stop [*geu-man*], bathroom [*hwa-jang-shill*], water [*mool*], hello [*an-young*], good-bye [*jal-ga*], thank you [*go-ma-wa*]). Although it sometimes takes a little time to understand what Jisoo wants or needs, Ms. Reeds thinks she is doing fairly well communicating with him. However, Ms. Reeds has noticed several incidents in class in which Jisoo was left alone or excluded by peers. She has also heard some of her students mimicking Jisoo's accent when speaking some words in English.

Questions to Explore Understanding of Children Who Speak Other Languages

Provide Simple Explanation: How many of you can speak more than one language or have family members who can speak more than one language? What languages are they? Who has traveled somewhere where people speak a language other than English? Where did you go, and what language was spoken? What was that like? Did you understand what people were saying? What did people do to help you get around and do the things you wanted to do, like order food, find your way around, or buy something? There are so many different languages that people use to talk with each other. Some people know one language, while others may learn to speak two, three, or even more languages!

Highlight Similarities: What language do you use? Do you have family members who speak a different language? If yes, what language?

Feelings: Have you ever said something that someone didn't understand? Or have you ever had someone say something to you that you did not understand? How did that make you feel? How does it feel when someone doesn't understand what you say or when you don't understand what someone else says?

Ideas: What do you think when you hear someone speaking in a language that you don't know? What do you know about the country of Korea and the language Jisoo speaks?

Actions: Jisoo's mom, dad, and grandma taught me to say some words in Korean. You could ask Jisoo to teach you some words in Korean, too. What might you do if you don't understand something that Jisoo says or if you think that Jisoo does not understand you? You could say it again, say it a different way, or use gestures.

Provide Positive Feedback: Learning a new language is fun! Now you and Jisoo can talk with each other in Korean *and* English.

Vignette 3: Conversations and Actions About Children from Diverse Racial and Ethnic Backgrounds

Sandra (age 7, Caucasian) is holding a Caucasian baby doll that she brought to class for show and tell. Sandra is showing the doll to other girls in the class when Aluel, a student who recently moved here from Kenya, approaches the group. Aluel asks if she can hold the baby doll. Sandra looks at Aluel and says, "You can't be a mommy to white babies. You can only be a mommy to black babies, so you can't hold her." Other girls in the group nod their head in agreement.

Questions to Explore Understanding of Children of a Different Race or Ethnicity

Provide Simple Explanation: People have many similarities and differences. Sometimes we notice that we have different skin color and different color eyes and hair. Even though we can see our different colors, we may share similar feelings and like many similar things.

Highlight Similarities: Look at each other's face. We all look different. Aluel's face is brown and Sandra's is lighter, but you both like playing with dolls!

Feelings: Aluel asked to hold the doll you brought, and you said "no." How do you feel when someone doesn't share with you?

Ideas: How do you think we get our skin, eye, and hair colors? Why do you think some children look very similar to their family members while other children do not?

Actions: Aluel likes dolls just like you. You could ask her if she has dolls at home, too, and what their names are.

Provide Positive Feedback: Have you seen parents who have skin, hair, or eye colors that are different from their babies? How would you describe your skin color? How would you describe your family members' skin colors? When babies are born, they become a blend of their parents' colors. Aluel could be a mommy to a baby with lighter skin, or her baby could have skin that looks just like her own. It is kind of you to share your doll with Aluel, because it doesn't matter if her skin color perfectly matches the baby doll's when she pretends to be the baby's mama.

Vignette 4: Conversations and Actions About Children from Diverse Family Structures

Jose (age 8, Hispanic) has a family that includes his mom, dad, and four siblings. He often speaks proudly of his grandparents who live with them. One day, he is looking at students' family photos that are posted on a wall near the dramatic play area. You notice him staring intently at one family photo. You move alongside him and say, "I see you're looking carefully at Will's family. What are you thinking?" Jose replies, "I see Will, his sister, and his daddy who drops him off, but who is that other guy? Where is his mommy? *¿Dónde está su madre? ¿Dónde está su abuela?*"

Questions to Explore Understanding of Children Who Have Different Family Structures

Provide Simple Explanation: There are many kinds of families. They may be like your family in some ways. They may be different from your family in some ways. Every family is a group of people who care about each other, and families are as different as the people who make them up. Not every family includes a mom and a dad. Some children live only with their mom, some children live with parents who are the same gender, and some children live with their grandparents. Let's take a look at these pictures together and have everyone introduce us to their families. Look at all your classmates with their family members in the pictures. Some families are big and others are small. What is your family like?

Highlight Similarities: Everyone you know lives in a family, and every family is different. They can be made up of many different family members. One thing we all have in common is that families are people who love and care for each other.

Feelings: How do you feel when you're doing something with your family? Let's ask Will what he likes most about his family.

Ideas: Who are Will's family members? Do we all have the same kind of family? Families are people who care for each other. Some families have one parent, while other families have two parents. Describe your family and the ways they show you that they care for you.

Actions: Ask Will to describe his family photo so you can learn more about his family. What does his family like to do together? How do they show that they care about him?

Provide Positive Feedback: There are all kinds of families. Some children have large families, and some children have small families. Some families have two parents, and some families have one parent. But no matter what kind of family you have, your family cares about you; your family is the place where you belong. It's nice of you to be curious about Will's family and the families of your classmates. Talk with your friends to learn more about the people they love and who love them.

PROFESSIONAL DEVELOPMENT

The four exercises presented in this chapter provided information about attitude formation, cultural influences on attitude development, perceptions about diversity, and diversity in classroom environments. In addition, the four vignettes provided examples of ways to respond to challenges likely to occur in diverse school settings. It is important to take a moment to ponder the following questions after reflecting on all of the exercises presented in this chapter. Following each question, we have provided some quotes from early childhood professionals with whom we have worked over the years. Their reflections, ideas, and plans for the future are insightful.

What can teachers learn about themselves that could inform their teaching practices and interactions with young children with differences in ability, language, ethnicity/race, and family structure?

- I realize that I have a lot of negative stereotypes that reflect my bias against people who grow up in poverty, most of whom represent minority populations. For example, when describing these students, I've often said, "poor thing," or "he can't help it, look at his parents," or "why should we expect more from those people?" It is now embarrassing to me that I conveyed negative and biased attitudes.

- I need to be better educated about people with disabilities. I often just pity them, which in reality is negative.

- I learned that I am afraid of white people and do not trust them. I need to work on this.

- The absence of conversation is powerful. It contributes to misunderstandings, fear, and negative attitudes.

What do teachers need to be cognizant of as they engage with children from diverse backgrounds and their families?

- I am now more sensitive to the words I use when discussing student issues with others.

- I need to be willing to change and grow in my understanding of differences.

- We are more alike than different.

What are examples of actions that teachers can take that have been informed by the research on attitude development?

- I now subscribe to *Teaching Tolerance*, which is free to teachers!

- I decided to lead a workshop at my school on the power of words and use myself as an example of what not to do. I hope it will lead to many good discussions among our faculty and staff.

How can teachers' newly acquired knowledge and skills be translated into behavior, decisions, and interactions with others?

- I definitely have learned that my class environment lacked materials, and because of this, I unintentionally gave negative messages about children from diverse backgrounds. I plan to change this in my own class.

- I am reviewing all of my communications with families to ensure that my words are respectful and inclusive.

- I formed a committee at school to address attitude development, using these tools with other teachers, and we have asked family members who represent diverse populations to be on our committee, too!

After discussing responses to these prompts, continue to Chapter 4 and begin reviewing how to set up a Making Friends program in your classroom.

Attitude Exercise

Directions: Identify an experience from your childhood that focused on an event, situation, or item that led you to have an early positive or negative perception and that over time shaped your attitude toward or against the event, situation, or item. Then answer the following questions:

1. What do you have a positive or negative attitude about?

2. What or who influenced, promoted, or lead you to having that attitude?

3. What were your *thoughts/ideas* about the event, item, or situation?

4. How did you *feel?* What were your *emotions or sensations?*

5. How was your *behavior* changed or altered because of that experience? How *did you act or what did you do* in this situation or event / in the presence of this item?

Remember Who You Are

Identify one or two *cultural identities* that shape who you are (shape the way you think and act). Who or what shaped these strong identities?	I am . . .	I am . . .
Name one or two *values or beliefs* that come from or are associated with your identities.	I believe or I value. . . .	I believe or I value. . . .
What were the *indirect experiences* that encouraged you to have these values and attitudes?		
What were the *direct experiences* that influenced you?		2.3.
What was the *overriding message* from your family?	I was told/taught that . . .	I was told/taught that . . .
How are *your behaviors still influenced* by your values?	I usually . . .	I usually . . .
How are your *expectations of others* influenced by your values and beliefs?	I expect others to . . .	I expect others to . . .

Unpack Your Perceptions About Diversity

Describe your early perceptions about diversity in terms of one of the following: disabilities, race/ethnicity, language, or family structure.

1. What are your earliest experiences/memories of someone with this difference?

2. Were the experiences positive or negative? What were the messages given to you about someone who has this difference?

3. Who gave you these messages, and how were the messages delivered?

4. How did those messages affect your early perceptions of individuals who were different from you? How did you think, feel, and act?

5. Do you still have those same ideas and feelings or engage in those same behaviors? If yes, how have your original perceptions been reinforced? If no, what happened to change them?

Diversity in School Environments (DSE)

Teacher: _____   Date: _____

Directions

- The DSE contains questions that enable teachers to describe the materials in their classroom and their school that depict individuals from diverse backgrounds (e.g., ability, race and ethnicity, language, and family structure). There are no right or wrong answers to the items on the DSE; the tool is simply meant to help you identify how individuals from diverse backgrounds are represented in your classroom and school.

- The DSE will take approximately 20 minutes to complete. It is divided into six sections:

  1. Classroom Environment: Visual and Aesthetic Elements
  2. Curriculum
  3. Books
  4. Dramatic Play
  5. Language
  6. Schoolwide Environment

- After completing the DSE, you may want to discuss your results with another teacher or an administrator who is familiar with your classroom setting. A trusted colleague may notice additional ways that you have represented diversity and may have suggestions for ways that you can increase representations of diversity.

- It will be helpful for you to revisit and rescore this tool periodically to reflect changes in your classroom and school environments.

How to Complete and Score the DSE

- Respond with "yes" or "no" to the questions about each aspect of diversity represented in your classroom.

- For each item that you answer "yes" to, consider adding examples to describe the material or activity that fulfills the requirement named in the item, as in this example:

	Y/N	Example
1. Are there images of children with disabilities in your room (e.g., photos or pictures reflecting people with differing abilities)?	Y	Poster of children with diverse abilities reading together—displayed in book center.

- All "yes" responses receive 1 point. All "no" responses receive 0 points. Further information about scoring is provided at the end of the DSE.

Section 1—Classroom Environment: Visual and Aesthetic Elements

Section 1A. Diversity in Your Classroom: *Disability*	Y/N	Example

1. Are there images of children with disabilities (e.g., photos or pictures reflecting people with differing abilities)?
  • If "NO," skip the remaining questions in Section 1A.
  • If "YES," complete Section 1A.		

2. Do these images reflect current life (are the photos or pictures up-to-date)?		
3. Indicate if these images have an adequate balance.		
a. Is there more than one person with a disability?		
b. Is there more than one type of disability represented?		
4. Do these images show differently abled people . . .		

	Y/N	Example
a. of various ethnic backgrounds?		
b. of various ages (adults and children)?		
c. doing work?		
d. engaging in recreational activities?		
e. with family members?		
f. in a positive way (active, independent)?		
Subtotal: Add the number of YES responses for Section 1A		

Section 1B: Diversity in Your Classroom: *Race and Ethnicity*	Y/N	Example
1. Are there images of children of different races/ethnicities (e.g., photos or pictures reflecting people of different races)? • If "NO," skip the remaining questions in Section 1B. • If "YES," complete Section 1B.		
2. Do these images reflect current life (are the photos or pictures up-to-date)?		
3. Indicate if these images have an adequate balance.		
a. Is there more than one person from a diverse race or ethnicity?		
b. Are there multiple races and ethnicities represented?		
4. Do these images show people from diverse racial and ethnic backgrounds . . .		
a. with a variety of abilities?		
b. of various ages (adults and children)?		
c. doing work?		
d. engaging in recreational activities?		
e. with family members?		
f. in a positive way (active, independent)?		
Subtotal: Add the number of YES responses for Section 1B		

Section 1C: Diversity in Your Classroom: *Family Structure*	Y/N	Example
1. Are there images of children from a variety of family structures (e.g., photos or pictures reflecting different family structures)? • If "NO," skip the remaining questions in Section 1C. • If "YES," complete Section 1C.		
2. Do these images reflect current life (are the photos or pictures up-to-date)?		
3. Indicate if these images have an adequate balance.		
a. Is there more than one person from a diverse family structure?		
b. Are there multiple family structures represented?		
4. Do these images show people from diverse family structures . . .		
a. with a variety of abilities?		
b. of various ages (adults and children)?		

	Y/N	Example
c. doing work?		
d. engaging in recreational activities?		
e. in a positive way (active, independent)?		
Subtotal: Add the number of YES responses for Section 1C		

Section 1D: Diversity in Your Classroom: *Language*	Y/N	Example
1. Are there images of children who use a variety of languages (e.g., photos or pictures reflecting different languages)? • If "NO," skip the remaining questions in Section 1D. • If "YES," complete Section 1D.		
2. Do these images reflect current life (are the photos or pictures up-to-date)?		
3. Indicate if these images have an adequate balance.		
a. Is there more than one person who uses a different language?		
b. Are there multiple languages represented (e.g., Spanish, sign language)?		
4. Do these images show people who use a different language or way of communicating . . .		
a. with a variety of abilities?		
b. of various ages (adults and children)?		
c. doing work?		
d. engaging in recreational activities?		
e. with family members?		
f. in a positive way (active, independent)?		
Subtotal: Add the number of YES responses for Section 1D		

Section 2—Curriculum

Diversity: *disability, race/ethnicity, language, family structure*	Y/N	Example
1. When images of people in different occupations are presented in your curriculum, are differently abled people represented?		
2. When images of important and/or famous individuals, past and present, are presented in your class curriculum, are differently abled people represented? If yes, who? Answer YES if more than two are named. Examples include Franklin Delano Roosevelt (polio), Helen Keller (visual and hearing impairment), Magic Johnson and Robin Williams (ADHD), Whoopi Goldberg and Tom Cruise (learning disability), and Stephen Hawking (ALS / Lou Gehrig's Disease).		
3. When images of people in different occupations are presented in your curriculum, are people from different races and ethnicities represented?		

	Y/N	Example
4. When images of important and/or famous individuals, past and present, are presented in your class curriculum, are different races and ethnicities represented? If yes, who? Answer YES if more than two are named. Examples include Barack Obama and Martin Luther King Jr. (African American), Cesar Chavez (Latino), Casimir Polaski (Polish), Yo-Yo Ma (Chinese), Squanto (Native American), and Apolo Anton Ohno (Japanese American).		
5. When images of people in different occupations are presented in your curriculum, are people who speak different languages represented?		
6. When images of important and/or famous individuals, past and present, are presented in your class curriculum, are people who speak different languages represented? If yes, who? Answer YES if more than two are named. Examples include Marlee Matlin and Heather Whitestone (American Sign Language), Jodie Foster (English, French, German, Spanish, Italian), Sammy Sosa (Spanish), Mila Kunis (English, Russian), Kobe Bryant (English, Italian), and Johnny Depp (English, French).		
7. When images of people in different occupations are presented in your curriculum, are different family structures represented?		
8. When images of important and/or famous individuals, past and present, are presented in your class curriculum, are people from different family structures represented? If yes, who? Answer YES if more than two are named. Examples include Toni Morrison, Coretta Scott King, and Jamie Foxx (single parent); Angelina Jolie, Dave Thomas, and Raven Symone (adoptive parents); and Neil Patrick Harris, Ellen DeGeneres, Rosie O'Donnell, and Guillermo Diaz (LGBT).		
Subtotal: Add the number of YES responses for Section 2		

Section 3—Books

Diversity: *disability, race/ethnicity, language, family structure*	Y/N	Example
1. Do children have access to books in your classroom that reflect children/adults with diverse abilities?		
2. Do children have access to books in your classroom that reflect children/adults from diverse racial and ethnic backgrounds?		
3. Do children have access to books in your classroom that reflect children/adults who use different languages? Answer YES if more than two languages are featured. Examples include sign language, braille, augmentative/alternative communication (AAC), and spoken/written languages other than English (e.g., French, Spanish, Vietnamese).		
4. Do children have access to books in your classroom that reflect diverse family structures? Answer YES if more than two family structures are featured. Examples include single parent families, adoptive families, foster families, families with incarcerated family members, and families with two moms or two dads.		
Subtotal: Add the number of YES responses for Section 3		

Section 4—Dramatic Play

Diversity: *disability, race/ethnicity, language, family structure*	Y/N	Example
1. Do children have access to tools/materials used by people with diverse abilities (e.g., crutches, braces, wheelchairs, walkers, canes, magnifying glasses, eyeglasses)?		
2. Do any dolls (bought or homemade) have different kinds of abilities?		
3. Do children have access to tools/materials used by people from various racial or ethnic backgrounds (e.g., food, cooking utensils, clothing or toys from different cultures)?		
4. Do any dolls (bought or homemade) represent different racial or ethnic backgrounds?		
5. Do children have access to tools/materials used by people who speak different languages or communicate in unique ways (e.g., toys and tools that "talk" in other languages, AAC devices, TTYs, braille typewriters, menus in a variety of languages)?		
6. Do any dolls (bought or homemade) represent different family structures (e.g., doll families with two moms or two dads, with grandparents as parents, with a single parent, or with biracial parents)?		
7. Do dolls (bought or homemade) reflect both genders?		
Subtotal: Add the number of YES responses for Section 4		

Section 5—Language

Diversity: *language, disability*	Y/N	Example
1. Do children have opportunities in your curriculum to see or use sign language, the Picture Exchange Communication System (PECS), and/or braille (e.g., labeling on furniture and materials, alphabet/number posters, songs, finger games)?		
2. Do children have opportunities in your curriculum to see or use spoken/written languages other than English (e.g., labeling on furniture and materials, alphabet/number posters, songs, finger games)?		
Subtotal: Add the number of YES responses for Section 5		

Section 6—Schoolwide Environment

Diversity: *disability, race/ethnicity, language, family structure*	Y/N	Example
1. Is there a schoolwide program that promotes and encourages interactions between children with and without disabilities?		
2. Is there a schoolwide unit/curriculum that provides information about children with disabilities?		
3. Are there schoolwide opportunities for children to see or use sign language, PECS, and/or braille (e.g., room or doorway labels)?		
4. Is there a schoolwide program that promotes and encourages interactions between children from diverse racial and ethnic backgrounds?		

5. Is there a schoolwide unit/curriculum that provides information about children from diverse racial and ethnic backgrounds?		
6. Are there schoolwide opportunities for children to see or use materials that represent diverse racial and ethnic backgrounds (e.g., culture fairs or assemblies, flags representing students' countries of origin)?		
7. Is there a schoolwide program that promotes and encourages interactions between children who speak different languages?		
8. Is there a schoolwide unit/curriculum that provides information about children who speak/write languages other than English?		
9. Are there schoolwide opportunities for children to see or use materials that represent written/spoken languages other than English (e.g., sing-along events including songs in other languages, exit signs, room labels)?		
10. Is there a schoolwide program that promotes and encourages interactions between children from different family structures?		
11. Is there a schoolwide unit/curriculum that provides information about children from a variety of family structures?		
12. Are there schoolwide opportunities for children to see or use materials that represent diverse family structures (e.g., access to LGBT books in the school library, opportunities to invite family members to school)?		
Subtotal: Add the number of YES responses for Section 6		

Section	Possible points	Points you earned
Classroom Environment: Visual and Aesthetic Elements		
Section 1A: Disability	10	
Section 1B: Race and Ethnicity	10	
Section 1C: Family Structure	9	
Section 1D: Language	10	
Curriculum		
Section 2	8	
Books		
Section 3	4	
Dramatic Play		
Section 4	7	
Language		
Section 5	2	
Schoolwide Environment		
Section 6	12	
Total	72	

Record your points for each section and then the total.

What does your total score indicate about the diversity in your classroom and school?

0   My classroom and school have *no representation* of diversity.

1–25   My classroom or school has *low representation* of diversity.

26–47   My classroom and school have *moderate representation* of diversity.

48–72   My classroom and school have *high representation* of diversity.

Concluding Thoughts

Congratulations on completing the DSE! Regardless of your score, you are doing something very valuable for your students by evaluating the ways you represent diversity in your classroom and school. Everyone has to start somewhere, and there is always room for improvement!

Now consider what your next steps will be to better represent diversity in your setting. Use your subtotal scores to identify areas where your classroom or school environment could be improved. Think about materials that you could add to your classroom or school environment, and use the resources found in Chapter 5 to locate materials needed.

Remember to revisit and rescore this tool periodically as you consider possible changes in your school and classroom environments.

Additional Comments and Ideas

Use this space to write down comments or ideas you have (e.g., ideas to share with colleagues, ideas of new ways to represent diversity in your classroom or school).

_____

_____

_____

_____

_____

_____

_____

_____

_____

_____

_____

_____

CHAPTER 4

Setting Up the Making Friends Program

TOOLBOX

(continued)

While the research behind the Making Friends program focuses on attitudes toward children with disabilities, the process for shaping attitudes can be applied to a wide range of diverse populations. For this reason, the program has been expanded to include promoting acceptance of differences related to disability, race/ethnicity, language, and family structure. These characteristics were selected because they represent the most common types of diversity in early childhood classes.

As discussed in Chapter 2, acceptance of differences is influenced by three primary sources: indirect experiences, direct experiences, and the primary social group. The Making Friends program is a literacy-based program that includes three components, which reflect these primary influences on attitudes:

- First, *the school literacy component provides indirect experiences* through reading children's books that include characters with differences related to disabilities, family structure, ethnicity and race, and linguistically diverse families. Guided discussions are used to highlight similarities between the characters in the book and children in the class and to dispel myths or misinformation about people who are different.

- Second, *the cooperative learning component provides direct experiences* with a variety of children (heterogeneously grouped) who are either classmates or from another class. This component can be structured as cooperative learning groups or cooperative play activities that are carefully organized to facilitate positive interactions with peers, using environmental arrangements. Environmental arrangements are generally thought of as the most natural strategy for supporting peer interactions and include methods such as arranging the physical space and monitoring the number of materials and children in each group so as to increase the likelihood of peer interactions. (For more details on environmental arrangements, see Odom & Brown, 1993; Sainato & Carta, 1992; Trawick-Smith, 1992.)

- Third, *the home literacy component involves the child's social group,* family members, in the reading of books and guided discussions at home. A young child's family represents the child's primary social group, whereas peers represent the child's secondary social group. Ideally, families are provided with one story per week and a guide for discussing the story

All the kids now seem to be much more accepting of kids with disabilities.
—Mrs. Tuten

that highlights similarities rather than differences. Peers are involved in the school literacy component and the cooperative play component.

In this chapter, each of these three components is discussed in greater detail with general guidelines for implementation, suggestions for applying universal design for learning (UDL) strategies to meet the needs of individual children, suggestions for how to schedule each component, suggestions for optimal implementation, and the criteria used for selecting books and materials. Specific ideas are provided to help teachers understand their role *before* starting each component to ensure purposeful planning, *during* each component to ensure active engagement of students, and *after* each component is completed to ensure reflective and responsive practice.

Before we look at the three components of the program, let's take a moment to think about universal design for learning. UDL sounds intimidating, but many teachers are already doing some of this as they plan for the diverse group of children in their classes. UDL is simply a formal way to assist teachers in planning ahead for diverse learners.

WHAT IS UNIVERSAL DESIGN FOR LEARNING?

I learned "bye"—how to sign "bye." I learned sign language.
—Antonia, 6 years old

UDL is a set of strategies that provides all individuals the opportunity to participate in an activity (CAST, 2011). In essence, the principles of UDL recognize that all individuals do not learn the same way. Thus, prior to the actual activity, teachers plan ahead by thinking about the following:

- Children's different ways of learning

- Multiple ways in which materials can be presented

- Different ways in which children can participate and demonstrate their knowledge

UDL is rooted in neuroscience, recognizing that when children are engaged in learning, they are utilizing three brain networks: a recognition network (the *what* of learning), a strategic network (the *how* of learning), and an affective network (the *why* of learning). An overview of these distinct ways in which children engage in learning is provided in Table 4.1 with examples for how to utilize UDL strategies to ensure that all children learn (CAST, 2011).

SCHOOL LITERACY COMPONENT

Most early childhood classrooms schedule time for a large-group meeting and book reading. An important part of the Making Friends program is the school literacy component. We suggest that you, the teacher, try to allot 15 minutes three times a week for a minimum of 6 weeks in the first half of the year, repeating this during the second half of the year, for the literacy component. This is an ideal schedule based on our research, but we understand the time constraints arising from the day-to-day realities in early childhood classes and encourage you to select a schedule for implementing the program that is feasible for your class, given your resources.

Table 4.1. Universal Design for Learning (UDL) overview

Network	Task	UDL strategy
Recognition network	The *what* of learning What facts do the children see, hear, and read? • What do they perceive? • What symbols or language do they utilize? • What do they comprehend?	Multiple means of representation • Present information in multiple ways. • Provide both visual and auditory ways to gain information. • Give attention to variances in language, such as by using multiple languages, symbols, and clarification of vocabulary. • Provide multiple levels of information and questions to address variance in comprehension.
Strategic network	The *how* of learning How do the children plan, perform tasks, and organize and express ideas?	Multiple means of action and expression • Allow children to express what they know in different ways to vary the response actions, such as by drawing, writing, or talking about the story. • Use different media for communication.
Affective network	The *why* of learning How do the children become engaged and stay motivated? What challenges, excites, and interests them?	Multiple means of engagement • Plan ahead and think of ways to spark motivation and interest. Foster interest by making topics personally and culturally relevant. • Plan ways to sustain interest and maintain attention. • Plan ways to challenge children who function on different levels.

> *The best part was that I had the opportunity to step back and watch my kids interact.*
> —*Mr. Johnson*

To help create a community of acceptance and foster positive attitudes toward all individuals, it is important that information is provided to children at a development level that is appropriate, that they feel comfortable asking questions, and that you focus on similarities while embracing and acknowledging differences.

Through a review process, using guidelines developed by Nasatir and Horn (2003), books that include characters with disabilities as well as books that include different family structures and ethnically, racially, and linguistically diverse families were critically evaluated, and books that were found to be positive in their portrayal of similarities and differences were selected. See Table 4.2 for a list of these books focusing on children who have disabilities; this list is simply a starting place. You can evaluate books using Nasatir and Horn's guidelines (Table 4.3) so that your pool of potential reading materials continues to grow. By adapting these guidelines (see Appendix 4.1), we have identified additional books about children from diverse backgrounds to get you started on building your class library of books on diversity (see Appendix 5.1).

General Guidelines for Setting Up the School Literacy Component

When planning, there are several things to keep in mind before, during, and after the school literacy component.

Table 4.2. Sample books with characters with disabilities

Book	Disability depicted
Let's Talk About Extraordinary Friends	General
Susan Laughs	Physical disability
Cookie	Communication
All Kinds of Friends	General
Sarah's Surprise	Communication
The Night Search	Visual impairment
Someone Special Just Like You	General
Be Quiet, Marina	Down syndrome
My Friend Isabelle	Down syndrome
We Can Do It!	General
We'll Paint the Octopus Red	Down syndrome
Ian's Walk	Autism
Andy and His Yellow Frisbee	Autism
Don't Call Me Special	General
Moses Goes to a Concert	Hearing impairment
Friends at School	General
Deaf Musicians	Hearing impairment
Can You Hear a Rainbow?	Hearing impairment

Table 4.3. Checklist for selecting books that portray disabilities appropriately

____ The story and illustrations respectfully depict people with disabilities while not promoting stereotypes (e.g., someone who is always pitied or is always a hero).

____ The story depicts characters with disabilities in various roles, balancing leadership roles and supporting roles of characters with and without disabilities.

____ Characters with disabilities are portrayed realistically, having similar experiences as people without disabilities.

____ The story uses current terminology and person-first language (e.g., "a child with Down syndrome" versus "a Down syndrome child"), avoiding offensive terms such as "slow" or "suffering from" when speaking about an individual with a disability or the disability itself.

____ The story was written relatively recently or can be adapted when read aloud to reflect more current language or knowledge (e.g., "an autistic child" can be adapted to "a child with autism").

____ The story was written and illustrated by individuals with knowledge of people with disabilities.

Source: Nasatir and Horn (2003).

Teacher's Role Before Storytime and Guided Discussion

1. Preread each book to be well versed in the storyline.

2. Prepare a range of questions that represent different levels and abilities. Each discussion guide should include a few questions that focus on comprehension, new vocabulary, and similarities and differences. Sample discussion guides are provided for books about children with disabilities (Figures 4.1 and 4.2), children from diverse racial backgrounds (Figure 4.3), children who use different languages (Figure 4.4), and children from diverse family structures (Figure 4.5). In addition, a blank template for creating discussion guides can be found in Appendix 4.2.

Bookmark Discussion Guide

Title: _We'll Paint the Octopus Red_

Author: _Stephanie Stuve-Bodeen_

Aspect of diversity: _Disability (Down syndrome)_

Content of the Story (select one or two questions, if time allows)
- What is the story about? _(a new baby boy named Isaac)_

- Why was the little girl upset about getting a new brother or sister? _(she didn't want to share her parents)_

- What did her dad say she could do with the baby to help out? _(change diapers, read, and play ball)_

- What did Isaac do when they went to visit Grandpa's farm? _(fed calves)_

Explanation of Diversity or Related Vocabulary
- _Down syndrome is something that causes differences in the way a baby looks and learns. No one can catch Down syndrome. A person is born with it._

- _Children like Isaac who have Down syndrome can do many things like you and me._

Similarities to Highlight
- How is Isaac in the story like you? _(there is nothing he cannot do; he just might take more time)_
- What arts and crafts do you like to do? _____
- Have you ever fed calves at a farm? Tell me about it. _____

Equipment, Materials, or Tools Related to Story Content
- None_____

Discussion Prompts
- Talk about what it might be like to play with a friend who has Down syndrome.
- _____

Thanks for taking 15 minutes to read and talk about this book with me!

Figure 4.1. Bookmark discussion guide for disability: _We'll Paint the Octopus Red._

Bookmark Discussion Guide

Title: Vamos a pintar el pulpo rojo

Autora: Stephanie Stuve-Bodeen

Discapacidad: Síndrome Down

Contenido del cuento (escoja 1 ó 2 preguntas si hay suficiente tiempo; opcional)

- ¿De qué se trata el cuento? (Un bebé nuevo que se llama Isaac).

- ¿Por qué le molestaba a la niña del cuento tener un hermanito o hermanita nueva? (No quería compartir a sus padres).

- ¿Qué dijo su papi que ella podría hacer con el bebé para ayudar? (Cambiarle los pañales, leer y jugar con la pelota).

- ¿Qué haría Isaac cuando fueran a la granja de su abuelito? (Dar de beber a becerros).

Explicación de la discapacidad o vocablos relacionados

- El síndrome Down es algo que causa diferencias en el aspecto de un bebé y su manera de aprender. Nadie puede contagiarse del síndrome Down; una persona nace así. Los niños como Isaac que tienen el síndrome Down pueden hacer muchas cosas como tú y yo.

-

Enfatice lo que tienen en común

- ¿De qué maneras es Isaac, el niño del cuento, como tú? (No hay nada que no pueda hacer, pero puede tardar más).
- ¿Cuáles actividades de arte y artesanías te gustan hacer?
- ¿Has dado de beber a becerros en una granja alguna vez? Cuéntamelo.

Equipos relacionados al contenido del cuento

- Ninguno

Experiencias del Grupo Cooperativo de Aprendizaje

- Cuéntame cómo te va con tus amigos en el Grupo Cooperativo de Aprendizaje en la escuela.

- ¿Quiénes jugaron contigo? ¿A qué jugaron?

Aliente la conversación. Trate temas que surjan, como maneras de jugar con un amigo que no puede ver u oír, que tarda más tiempo en hacer cosas, etc.

¡Gracias por apartar un rato para leer y contar este libro conmigo!

Figure 4.2. Bookmark discussion guide for disability: *We'll Paint the Octopus Red* (in Spanish).

Bookmark Discussion Guide

Title: Black Is Brown Is Tan

Author: Arnold Adoff

Aspect of diversity: Race and culture (biracial family)

Content of the Story (select one or two questions, if time allows)
- What is the story about? (a brother and sister who have an African American mom and a Caucasian dad)
- What do the children like to do with their parents? (snuggle in bed, eat together, sing together)
- What does the dad do outside? (cut wood for the fire, cook corn and hamburgers)
- What do the grandmas do when they visit? (kiss the girl and boy on the cheek)

Explanation of Diversity or Related Vocabulary
- The author uses many words to describe skin tones. The words are nice to hear and tell us about all the different colors that are in people's skin, hair, and eyes (i.e., coffee, pumpkin pie, ginger red, light with pinks and tiny tans).
-

Similarities to Highlight
- How are the children in the story like you? (they like to spend time with their mom, dad, and grandmas)
- What do you like to do with the person who takes care of you?
- Have you ever written a poem to describe someone who you love? Tell me about it.

Equipment, Materials, or Tools Related to Story Content
- None

Discussion Prompts
- Talk about what it might be like to play with a friend who is a different race than you are or who has parents that look different from each other.
-

Thanks for taking 15 minutes to read and talk about this book with me!

Figure 4.3. Bookmark discussion guide for racial diversity: *Black Is Brown Is Tan.*

Bookmark Discussion Guide

Title: My Way / A mi manera

Author: Lynn Reiser

Aspect of diversity: Language (Spanish)

Content of the Story (select one or two questions, if time allows)
- What is the story about? (two girls who play together)

- What things does each girl like to do "her way"? (fix her hair, make art, take a nap)

- Where do the girls play together? (at school)

- What does each girl say at the end of the book? (that she always likes to do things with her friend)

Explanation of Diversity or Related Vocabulary
- The book is written in two languages, English and Spanish. The first girl describes what she likes to do in English, and the second girl describes what she likes to do in Spanish. The illustrations help us see how they do things differently.

-

Similarities to Highlight
- How are the girls in the story like you? (they greet their friends, like to make art, and eat lunch at school)
- What things do you like to do your own way? _____
- Have you ever tried to do something a friend's way? Tell me about it. _____

Equipment, Materials, or Tools Related to Story Content
- None_____

Discussion Prompts
- Talk about what it might be like to play with a friend who speaks a different language than you do. _____

-

Thanks for taking 15 minutes to read and talk about this book with me!

Figure 4.4.   Bookmark discussion guide for language diversity: *My Way / A mi manera.*

Bookmark Discussion Guide

Title: _We All Have Different Families_

Author: _Melissa Higgins_

Aspect of diversity: _Family structure (different kinds of families)_

Content of the Story (select one or two questions, if time allows)
- What is the story about? (different types of families)

- What are some different types of families? (big families, small families, families with two dads)

- How do the people in each family look in the pictures? (happy, they are smiling)

- What are some words you learned at the end of the book? (divorced, foster parents, stepmom)

Explanation of Diversity or Related Vocabulary
- This book describes some new words children might not know. When a parent adopts a child, he or she becomes a new parent to someone else's child. When a person is divorced, he or she is not married anymore. A stepparent (stepmom or stepdad) is a parent's new spouse. If someone's stepmom or stepdad has a child already, that person is their stepbrother or stepsister.

- _____

Similarities to Highlight
- How are the children in the story like you? (they like to spend time with their family)
- What words would you use to describe your family? _____
- Who are the people in your family? _____
- What is special about your family? _____

Equipment, Materials, or Tools Related to Story Content
- None_____

Discussion Prompts
- Talk about what it might be like to play with a friend whose family is different from yours. _____

- _____

Thanks for taking 15 minutes to read and talk about this book with me!

Figure 4.5. Bookmark discussion guide for family diversity: _We All Have Different Families._

Discussion guides should include questions about the following:

- Key content from the story (*What is the story about? Why was her mommy upset when she saw Molly on the chair?*)

- Vocabulary (*What is sign language? What does it mean to be bilingual?*)

- Similarities between book characters and students (*How are the children in the story just like you? Who likes ice cream like the boy in the story? Who speaks more than one language like the girls in the story? Do any of you have friends at school like the girl in the story?*)

- Equipment presented in the story (*What is a wheelchair? Why do some people use it? What are braces? What is a communication board?*)

3. Select one to two questions per topic during each book reading, depending on time.

4. For ease of use, guided discussion cards can be placed within each book so that sample questions and comments are readily available to use during large-group book reading.

5. Also consider putting sticky notes on pages of the book as prompts for the questions to ask.

6. Review established rules and expectations for storytime. For example, do students have assigned seating? Do students need to raise their hand before asking or answering questions or making comments? Are there common phrases that need to be used, such as *crisscross applesauce* for seating?

7. Use a gathering song or routine to foster a smooth transition and focus children's attention on large-group storytime.

Teacher's Role During Storytime and Guided Discussion

1. Make sure children are seated comfortably and know the expectations for book reading and discussion.

2. Strategically seat all children so they can hear and see the book and pictures so that no one feels isolated or left out of the reading circle.

3. Read with great enthusiasm and affect, raising and lowering your voice to match the story content, while interspersing opportunities for children to comment or ask questions as the story progresses.

4. Read at a pace that matches students' needs and the content of the story. Use expectant pauses to highlight the climax of a story and speed up the pace as indicated by the story content or students' reactions.

5. Encourage conversations and help children focus on similarities while also acknowledging, celebrating, and discussing differences.

We learned about sharing with my friends.
—*Matt, 5 years old*

6. Address issues that arise, such as a book character's communication difficulties. For instance, should a student wonder how he might communicate with someone who is deaf, you might suggest that he could learn some sign language or use gestures. You could then engage all students in a discussion of how they might gain such skills.

7. Rotate questions among students so everyone has a chance to respond to a question or provide a comment or opinion.

Teacher's Role After Storytime and Guided Discussion

Transition times can be hectic for young children as they shift to the next activity, such as cooperative learning groups. Here are a few suggestions that may ensure smooth transitions.

1. Compliment children for their participation and attention during storytime, encouraging them to "pat themselves on the back" for doing a great job listening.

2. Take a moment to bend and stretch with a song.

3. To ease students into their cooperative learning groups, provide transition statements such as the ones in Table 4.4, which provide them with ideas for the cooperative learning.

Universal Design for Learning for the School Literacy Component

When preparing for the school literacy component, it is important to plan for children with different learning needs (see Figure 4.6).

Day One

Today we read *Andy and His Yellow Frisbee*, about a boy with autism. Now we are going to play with farmhouses and people with and without disabilities or special needs. What are some things you could do? You can pretend to feed the farm animals with a friend or go for a walk around the farm with a friend. Great, now let's go have fun. Remember to use your words to ask a friend to share.

Day Two

Today we read *Don't Call Me Special*, about children with disabilities or special needs. Now we are going to play with dinosaurs, water, and water tools in sensory bins! What are some things you could do? You can pretend to help dinosaurs swim and play games in the water, or you can pretend to give the dinosaurs a shower with a friend! Great, now let's go have fun. Remember to use your words to ask a friend to share.

Day Three

Today we read *Moses Goes to a Concert*, about children who are deaf or have hearing impairments. Now we are going to play with our friends. We are going to pretend we are at the grocery store. What are some things you can do? You can pretend to buy food items, or you can be the grocery store worker or a customer who wants to buy food with a friend! Great, now let's go have fun. Remember to use your words to ask a friend to share.

Table 4.4. Transition statements between storytime cooperative learning activities

UDL →	Multiple means of representation	Multiple means of engagement	Multiple means of action and expression
Planning ↓	Use various *formats/structures* within instructional and learning activities with differences in *task complexity and/or expectations* in response to different ability levels and *different ways children learn and communicate.*	Use multiple means to *motivate* children; *obtain and maintain attention* in response to different learning styles and challenges, interests, and preferences.	Plan for *variety in response modes to demonstrate skills* in response to different ability levels, reflecting different ways in which individuals organize and express skill/knowledge.
Reading and listening to stories	• Present story with spoken word, sign language, or in movie format. • Present the story using multiple formats (e.g., pictures from book, flannel board symbols, alternate vocabulary).	• Allow children to hold their own book. • Allow children to use sensory objects as appropriate during large-group time.	• Plan for active listening with participation based on high frequency word from the story (e.g., "Each time you hear *butterfly*, make a flying butterfly.") • Vary students' listening stance based on their needs—some stand, sit, or lay down to show they are listening.
Responding to guided discussions	• Plan specific questions for specific children with differing abilities, so all can participate. • Vary timing of questions, having some independent and some that build on one another.	• Some responses can be motor movements; other responses can be verbal. • Some responses can be in Spanish, while other responses can use English or sign language.	• Some students can use a communication board, PECS, or sign language. • Include some whole-group responses, such as clapping, hand signals, or sign language.

Figure 4.6. Applying universal design for learning to the school literacy component.

UDL Tips: Listening to the Story

1. Plan how to utilize teaching assistants, adult volunteers, student teachers, or related service personnel who are available during the school literacy component.

   • If other adults are present during storytime, strategically position them in the reading circle. Ask one-to-one assistants, teaching assistants, and volunteers to be seated among the children, for they can be a second set of hands (and laps), if needed.

   • Explain to adults that they should have an invisible presence. It is important to stress that their presence should not interrupt or interfere with the story or discussion but rather quietly support children in attending.

   • Consider asking one adult to sit with a child with an additional copy of the book for the child and adult to hold and view during reading, if this level of support seems necessary. Strategically seat all children, especially children with disabilities, in positions that will optimize their experience (such as next to or in the lap of a teaching assistant or one-to-one aide, or at the front or edge of the group). If it has not already been determined which position works best for a child, try out different locations within the group and evaluate how they work. Consider the following: Are children allowed to sit anywhere, or are they expected to sit on carpet squares or predetermined spaces? Do some children sit in adapted chairs, beanbag

Children are a lot better about helping each other and knowing they need to share.
—Ms. Young

chairs, or other special seats that need to be available and arranged prior to the start of large-group time?

2. Consider using sensory objects, if appropriate. Can children have sensory or transitional objects (e.g., squish balls) during structured activities such as large-group time? Will a timer be used to signal the end of storytime, or will the time allocated vary from day to day depending on children's engagement and your schedule for that day?

3. Create ways to increase active listening and participation whereby children are encouraged to make a motor movement or a sound each time they hear a high-frequency word from the story. For example, say, "Each time you hear me say *butterfly* in the story, make a flying butterfly" (cross hands at the wrist with palms facing your face, interlock thumbs, wave fingers, and move arms up), or "Moo each time I read the word *cow*." Note that because reading time is relatively brief, it is important to select only one or two simple motor behaviors.

4. Utilize specialized materials (e.g., visuals supports, adapted books) as needed, remembering to use the least-to-most hierarchy (Meadan, Ostrosky, Santos, & Snodgrass, 2013). If needed, consult with other team members (e.g., physical therapists, occupational therapists) to determine supports for individual children. For example, one child may be provided with communication cards by her speech and language therapist so she can quietly ask questions of the teaching assistant while the story is read. This adjustment enables her to more fully participate in the story.

5. If the text of the book appears too dense or long for a particular group of students, consider ways to summarize, condense, or skim sections of the book. There is no rule that requires a teacher to read a book word for word from beginning to end!

UDL Tips: Guided Discussion

1. Tag pages with sticky notes to intersperse questions as the story is read. Plan questions for specific children, reflecting their ability levels. Place the names of the children on the notes with the questions to ensure that all children have a chance to successfully respond to a question.

2. Consider multiple ways to encourage children's involvement throughout the story and discussion.

   - Some answers might be given as choral responses (i.e., a repeated refrain might be said in unison). For example, when you ask, "What day was it?" all of the students can say, "It was her birthday."

   - Encourage children to share information with a classmate sitting near them (e.g., "Everyone tell a friend near you about your favorite food.").

   - Encourage children to give nonverbal responses (e.g., "Everyone wiggle your thumb if you like to

I watched children with special needs [in my classroom] become more verbal.
—*Ms. Salo*

play soccer. Now, pat your head if you like baseball. And touch your nose if you like to swim.").

- Establish a method for whole-group responding using sign language or signals (e.g., use signs for *yes* or *no* responses or a signal such as thumbs-up for agree and thumbs-down for disagree so children can respond to questions such as "Have you ever stayed in a hotel?" or "Can you speak more than one language?").

- Accept multiple ways of responding, such as combining a motor response with verbal response, using a motor response instead of a verbal response, or using picture symbols (hand held) or an easel (so everyone can see a common communication system). Using a communication system (e.g., symbols, pictures, words) with the whole class enables all children to become familiar with the communication system used by a few children and thus increases the use and understanding of it across the whole class.

Scheduling the School Literacy Component

When planning a book reading schedule, consider a 3-day-per-week rotation that first includes a book with more general information (e.g., the characters in the book have a range of disabilities), followed by 2 days of book reading that focus on more specific disabilities (e.g., visual impairments, autism, Down syndrome, deafness). See the sample rotation in Table 4.5.

COOPERATIVE LEARNING COMPONENT

Most early childhood teachers schedule time for cooperative learning or cooperative play. This is an essential part of the Making Friends program, where children participate in carefully planned experiences with children who have differences related to disabilities, race/ethnicity, language, or family structure. After storytime is complete, children make the transition into small cooperative learning groups (CLGs).

The CLGs are semistructured social playgroups of children who are provided with carefully selected materials that have a high social element or value to them as well as some materials that depict diversity (e.g., individuals of other races, individuals with disabilities, adaptive equipment). The activities for this component are designed to support socialization among small groups of children.

It is important to ensure that children in the CLGs both become engaged in the activity and socialize with one another. The materials need to be both familiar and enticing to children. To address this need, it is important to rotate materials just as the books are rotated. As Table 4.5 shows, books and materials are rotated to ensure novelty and interest. Creating this rotation schedule ahead of time enables class volunteers and teaching assistants to help put the materials together prior to the CLGs. Note that the chart also includes examples of cooperative motor play. Some classes may prefer to implement classwide motor play activities to foster a sense of belonging among the whole class. These activities should lend themselves to enabling everyone in the class to fully participate.

Table 4.5.   Sample rotation of books and materials

Date	Week	Book	Disability	Character gender	Cooperative learning groups	Cooperative motor play
Sept. 29		Begin preparing materials				
Oct. 21	1	1. *Let's Talk About Extraordinary Friends*	General	Both	House with people with and without disabilities	Parachute play
Oct. 22		2. *Susan Laughs*	Physical	Female	Cars and trucks with people with and without disabilities, blocks	Parachute play
Oct. 23		3. *Cookie*	Communication	Female	Playdough with cutters and scissors	Parachute play
Oct. 28	2	4. *All Kinds of Friends*	General	Both	Farm with people with and without special needs, blocks	Kick ball
Oct. 29		5. *Sarah's Surprise*	Communication	Female	Sensory bins with dinosaurs, sand, pouring tools	Kick ball
Oct. 30		6. *The Night Search*	Visual impairment	Female	Cooking and eating toys with food and stoves with dolls with disabilities	Kick ball
Nov. 3	3	7. *Someone Special Just Like You*	General	Both	Doctor kits with dolls with special needs	Soccer
Nov. 5		8. *Be Quiet, Marina*	Down syndrome	Female	Mrs. and Mr. Potato Head with mirrors, Wikki Stix	Soccer
Nov. 6		9. *My Friend Isabelle*	Down syndrome	Female	Restaurant: stove, food, telephones, cash registers, money, menus	Soccer
Nov. 10	4	10. *We Can Do It!*	General	Both	House with people with and without disabilities	Obstacle course
Nov. 12		11. *We'll Paint the Octopus Red*	Down syndrome	Both	Cars and trucks with people with and without disabilities, blocks	Obstacle course
Nov. 13		12. *Ian's Walk*	Autism	Male	Playdough with birthday party theme: pegs, candles, hats	Obstacle course
Nov. 17	5	13. *Andy and His Yellow Frisbee*	Autism	Male	Farm with people with and without disabilities, blocks	T-ball or Whiffle ball
Nov. 18		14. *Don't Call Me Special*	General	Both	Sensory bins with dinosaurs, sand, water, water tools	T-ball or Whiffle ball
Nov. 19		15. *Moses Goes to a Concert*	Hearing impairment	Male	Grocery store: food, money, cash registers	T-ball or Whiffle ball
Nov. 21	6	16. *Friends at School*	General	Both	Doctor kits with animals with special needs	Parachute play
Nov. 24		17. *Moses Goes to School*	Hearing impairment	Male	Mrs. and Mr. Potato Head with mirrors, pipe cleaners	Parachute play
Nov. 25		18. *Can You Hear a Rainbow?*	Hearing impairment	Male	Dress up, community helpers, stove, food, telephones, cash register	Parachute play
Dec. 1		Celebrate with a closing activity				

In addition, it is important to give careful attention to which materials and activities are selected for any given program. The purpose of cooperative learning or cooperative play is for children to have positive experiences as they engage in fun activities with children in their class who are different from them with regard to gender, abilities, race/ethnicity, language, or family structure. Therefore, to ensure heterogeneity in the groupings of children, during the planning time ensure that diversity is represented in each play or learning group. In addition, it is important to choose activities that are known to support social interactions. Angie, a first-grade teacher, completed a checklist (Figure 4.7) before her students engaged in a restaurant activity. As can be seen from her responses, the materials met all of the criteria on the checklist and were likely to lead to many social interactions among her students. These types of classroom activities can be interspersed with motor games such as parachute play, kick ball, and T-ball that involve the whole class in teamwork. Appendix 4.3 will allow you to evaluate materials and activities to ensure that cooperative learning groups have high social value.

General Guidelines for Setting Up the Cooperative Learning Component

When planning the cooperative learning component for a class, there are several things to keep in mind before, during, and after the cooperative learning component. The purpose of this component is for students to have positive direct experiences with peers who are different from them.

Teacher's Role Before Cooperative Learning

1. Think carefully about how children will be grouped to ensure that each small group has a mix of children representing differences with

---

Angie's First Grade Class: Restaurant with picture menus in English and Spanish, plates, utensils, pretend food (pizza, tacos, sushi)

The Materials and Toys . . .

✓	Allow some manipulation but are not so intricate as to require one child's whole attention
✓	Depict variety of races, gender and abilities *No, but foods represent different cultures and use of multiple languages*
✓	Include an element of socio-dramatic play or items that might be adapted for socio-dramatic play. For example, toys or materials with high social value that are easy to make up stories such as grocery store, restaurant, cooking and eating
✓	Encourage interactions among children and questions to each other about the materials
✓	Require one child to help others in playing or operating (either physical assistance or verbal instructions) such as with parachute play, T ball, veterinarian visit, grocery store
✓	Have a number of parts but not so many parts that the majority of the time will be spent in examining all of the pieces. A small number of parts will also promote students to share
✓	Will maintain the students' attention for the entire length of the cooperative play
✓	Will promote mutual use by 2 or more students
✓	Are the appropriate size for children with different abilities
✓	Are developmentally appropriate for the target audience

Figure 4.7. Criteria for selecting of materials. (From Favazza, P.C, LaRoe, J., & Odom, S.L. [1999]. *Special friends: A manual for creating accepting environments.* Boulder, CO: Roots & Wings.)

regard to gender, disability, race/ethnicity, language, and family structure. Also, think about children's traits to ensure that children with strengths in interpersonal relationships are paired with children who struggle in this area.

2. Ideally, if a class consists of 24 students, there would be four groups of six diverse students.

3. Select materials using the toys and materials selection criteria in Appendix 4.3, or use materials that are known to have high social value. For example, some materials are designed for individual use (e.g., small puzzles, single-seat rocking boat), which provides limited opportunity for social interactions. Other materials have high social value, as they are designed for cooperative play (e.g., dramatic play materials, large floor puzzles, sensory bins) and they foster social interactions among several children.

4. Prepare bins with materials for the day, making sure each CLG receives the same materials.

5. Limit the number of materials in the bins to ensure that children need to share and take turns. For example, if a water activity is used, provide three to four pouring toys (in addition to other water toys) for six children to encourage interaction among peers.

6. Students should typically remain in the same group for the duration of the program to foster relationships among group members.

7. Each teacher and teaching assistant (or volunteer, student teacher, etc.) should be responsible for supervising (and, if needed, providing support to) one to two CLGs.

8. Tell the children what materials they have to play with for the 15-minute cooperative learning group. Provide transition statements and prompts to get them thinking about what they might do with the materials, such as the following:

   "Today we are playing with blocks."

   "What do you think you could do today with the farm toys?"

   "We have food and menus to play with in our groups; who can share an idea of what you might do?"

9. If the children struggle to come up with ideas, provide suggestions as needed, such as the following:

   "You might use the blocks to build a garage for the cars."

"You might work together to build a fence to keep the farm animals in."

"You might pretend to be at a restaurant and be servers and customers."

Teacher's Role During Cooperative Learning

1. Set the timer for 15 minutes, telling the children that when the timer goes off, they need to clean up.

2. Walk away from the groups (standing several feet away) and intervene only if needed so as not to intrude on children's social interactions. Do not prompt social interactions or praise children (unless this is part of a child's behavioral support plan).

3. Redirect children back to their cooperative learning group if they wander away.

Teacher's Role After Cooperative Learning

1. When the timer goes off, thank the children for playing so well with their friends.

2. Sing a song for cleanup to focus attention on everyone putting away materials.

3. If there is time, ask children to talk about the ways they found to play with their friends.

Universal Design for Learning for the Cooperative Learning Component

The key to a successful cooperative learning group is the full participation of *all* children. This will require thoughtful reflection on which group members may work well together and thinking ahead about the elements of the CLGs that may need adjustments for all children to be full participants.

UDL Tips: Materials and Activities

1. Preview all materials and activities prior to using them to ensure the success of all children with all materials.

2. Substitute items that may present challenges or issues.

3. Offer substitute items to all children in all CLGs so as not to single out a child with special needs (e.g., shredded paper used as a substitute for dirt for children who might not enjoy playing in dirt).

4. Ensure that materials are distributed on tables in such a way that they can be reached by all children.

UDL Tips: Seating

1. When possible, remove chairs to encourage movement and socialization around assigned areas, unless a child needs seating because of special needs.

2. If adaptive seating is utilized, ensure that children with special needs are still in close proximity to other CLG members.

3. If possible, substitute the use of a wheelchair lap tray for the table that everyone else is using. In this way, all children are seated at one large table, in close proximity to one another.

UDL Tips: Interactions Among Peers

1. Use pretransition statements to prepare all children for the next activity. Pretransition statements also can be an opportunity to encourage children to share and work cooperatively in CLGs.

2. Stand on the edge of the CLGs, close enough to monitor but far enough away that children are playing on their own, without adult intrusion. We typically encourage teachers to move about on the edge of groups, trying to be invisibly present.

3. When children seek adult attention for solving problems, redirect them to seek assistance from members of their CLG so that all children become used to helping one another and talking to one another to resolve differences.

4. If a child has a special way of communicating (e.g., bilingual, sign language, communication cards), explain this to other children in the CLG, and integrate it into the other aspects of class discussion to promote classwide understanding and use.

5. If it is necessary to discuss a child's unique needs with the whole class, obtain parent permission to do so. Sometimes family members may want to talk to the class about their son or daughter, as they can be excellent resources in explaining the child's unique strengths and needs. However, make sure that any conversation about children does not draw negative attention to them.

UDL Tips: Connecting Family Members to the CLG

1. Communicate to families (through weekly newsletters or e-mail) in their home language about children who are in their child's CLG. Use the names of the classmates so family members can have a conversation with their child about the playgroup.

2. Communicate with families about the play materials so they know the types of play that took place and can use words or pictures that help their child talk about cooperative learning and at the same time incorporate the multiple languages used in school. For example, on sand play days, children may be given big and little shovels, small buckets, dinosaurs, and little people figures. A newsletter to families could include words and pictures that represent these objects to encourage conversations with their children. A sample chart for using UDL strategies during CLG time is provided in Figure 4.8.

Scheduling the Cooperative Learning Component

When planning for cooperative learning or designing a cooperative play schedule, allot 15–20 minutes three times a week for a minimum of

UDL →	Multiple means of representation	Multiple means of engagement	Multiple means of action and expression
Activity ↓	Use various *formats/structures* within instructional and learning activities with differences in *task complexity and/or expectations* in response to different ability levels and *different ways children learn and communicate.*	Use multiple means to *motivate* children; *obtain and maintain attention* in response to different learning styles and challenges, interests, and preferences.	Plan for *variety in response modes to demonstrate skills* in response to different ability levels, reflecting different ways in which individuals organize and express skill/knowledge.
House and people with and without disabilities	• Provide people of various races, genders, and abilities. • Provide a house with various levels, rooms, and materials to depict different functions for different roles that may be played out.	• Provide ample choices of materials so children can demonstrate autonomy—but not so many choices that children do not need to engage with one another to share. • Encourage children to engage in the selection of household materials to be included. • Minimize distractions.	• Present the layout of the house in various formats on different days. • Provide materials that lend themselves to goal setting within cooperative play (e.g., cooking materials may lend to cooking, bathing materials to bathing dolls).
Cars, trucks, and blocks with people with and without disabilities	• Provide wide variety in materials (various sizes of blocks, cars, trucks for ease in manipulation). • Provide people of various races, genders, and abilities.	• Engage children in the selection of trucks and people to be included. • Minimize distractions. • Provide fewer cars than children to promote engagement with one another.	• Provide materials such as a road for children needing additional scaffolding to demonstrate skill. • Set up materials in a manner that looks authentic to a scene with cars and trucks to provide a jump-start to organizing them.
Playdough with cutters and scissors	• Provide a variety of cutting tools and different colors of playdough. • Provide various cutters or materials that can roll out playdough in various ways.	• Engage children in the selection of cutters to be included. • Minimize distractions. • Provide fewer cutters than children to promote engagement with one another.	• Use various table-top materials such as rough and smooth surfaces to allow for varied experience. • Model ways to use materials to provide ideas for skill demonstration.

Figure 4.8. Applying universal design for learning to cooperative learning group activities.

6 weeks in the first half of the year, and then repeat this during the second half of the year.

HOME LITERACY COMPONENT

The third part of the Making Friends program is the home literacy component. This component is very important, as it provides families with a way to get involved at home in the discussions about diversity.

To help establish continuity and consistency between school and home activities, the home literacy component should be developed using the same premises as the school literacy component: building a community of acceptance and fostering positive attitudes toward individuals with differing abilities. Similar to the focus in the classroom, it is important that information at home is provided to children at a developmental level that is appropriate, that they feel comfortable asking questions, and that family members focus on similarities while embracing and acknowledging differences. Teachers can share information with family members about book reading experiences using a home communication letter. Two examples of home communication letters (one in English, one in Spanish) are provided in Appendixes 4.4 and 4.5; these can be adapted for use in any classroom.

We have long known that book reading at home is a popular literacy activity for children and their family members to enjoy together (Dickinson, 2001). This activity engages the family in the child's school activities and provides a wonderful routine for building strong family relationships in this shared experience.

The Making Friends program supports this home reading activity by providing books for children to read with family members. Each week at school, students listen to and discuss three books about diversity related to race/ethnicity, disability, language, or family structure. On the third day of each week, children take home one of the books that was read that week at school to read and discuss it with family members. The same discussion guides used at school are inserted into each book to facilitate conversations at home. All discussion guides highlight the similarities between people while celebrating their differences.

General Guidelines for Setting Up Home Literacy Component

Teacher's Role Before the Home Literacy Component

1. To help promote family participation in book reading activities, information should be shared with families ahead of time regarding the importance of engaging in literacy (book reading or storytelling) activities at home with their children. Teachers may already share information about home literacy through weekly newsletters or other forms of communication with families. It is important that this information is provided in family-friendly language that avoids jargon or terms that may be unfamiliar to families.

2. Books should be sent home at the end of the third day for each of the 6 weeks. In order to prepare books for home dissemination, plastic reusable bags can be used to organize each book with a bookmark discussion guide and parent and child reading record. Books can be prepared ahead of time, and on the day they will be disseminated, they can be placed in three separate stacks in close proximity to the teacher to make it easy for children to select one.

3. Teachers can decide to disseminate books either after completion of the cooperative learning activity or during any other time of the day that works. A song or routine can be used to help gather children's attention. If books are distributed at the end of the day before children get ready to go home, it is important to remind children what books they read during the week, why they are taking the books home, and that they need to return them after reading them with their families.

4. Have stacks of books ready (about 8–10 copies per book, depending on the number of children in the classroom), and tell children that if their first choice of a book is not available, they can make another choice.

5. There are several ways to organize children to choose a book to bring home:

- Children can line up or remain seated while their names are called to pick a book. It is important to call different children or groups of children to go first each week to increase the likelihood that all of the children in the class will at some point be able to bring home their first-choice book. Make sure that children are comfortable and know the expectations for waiting and for making choices. If children need assistance or accommodations in order to choose a book, make sure they are provided with the appropriate supports to successfully do so.

- If teaching assistants, class volunteers, student teachers, or related service personnel are available during the time children will be choosing books to bring home each week, consider how to best involve them. They can help children line up and get ready to choose a book, they can help record which book each child chose to bring home, or they can help children put books in their cubbies or backpacks. They may also help children who need assistance or additional time to put their chosen book away. Communicate to the assisting adults that they should support children, but they should not be making choices for children or "doing the work" for them. Rather, they should gently guide children to participate in the book dissemination section of the day and use supports that will optimize children's learning (e.g., verbal or visual prompts).

- As children are called to choose a book to bring home, record their choice on a chart that family members initial and return with the book. See the completed parent and child reading record (Figure 4.9). Blank parent and child reading records (in English and Spanish) are provided in Appendixes 4.6 and 4.7.

    Bookmarks with discussion guides can be placed within each book to provide family members with sample questions and comments to use during home book reading. Each bookmark should be adapted from the guided discussion used for the school literacy component. Like the one used at school, the bookmark includes questions related to the following:

    - Key content from the story (*What was the boy's name in the story? What was Andy's favorite thing to do in the story?*)

    - Vocabulary (*Some children use sign language; what is sign language? Some children are bilingual; what does it mean to be bilingual? Sometimes, a translator helps Cindy. What is a translator?*)

    - Similarities between the book characters and students (*The boy in the story can do many things just like you. What are some of the things he can do? The girl in story likes ice cream. Do you like ice cream too?*)

    - Equipment presented in the book (*What is a wheelchair? Why do some people use it? What is a communication board?*)

Child's name: _Cameron_____   Teacher's name: _Mr. Jenkins_____

Parent and Child Reading Record

Dear Parent or Guardian,

This form will enable us to keep up with the home reading component of the Making Friends program. Please keep this form in your child's Ziplock bag until the program is complete.

All of the stories that your child chooses to bring home will be listed below across the 6-week program. When you have read and discussed each story with your child, place your initials in the middle column. Record any comments you have about the story in the last column. Return the book and this record at the beginning of every week.

Thank you!

	Story title	Parent initials	Comments
Week 1	Let's Talk About Extraordinary Friends	JF	We loved this book!
Week 2	Susan Laughs	JF	Another great one.
Week 3	We Can Do It!	JF	Very positive book.
Week 4	We'll Paint the Octopus Red	JF	
Week 5	The Night Search	JF	Great one for talking about blindness.
Week 6	All Kinds of Friends, Even Green!	JF	Oops! We forgot to read it. Please send it back!

Figure 4.9. Sample parent and child reading record.

Encourage family members to select one or two questions from each topic during each book reading.

Teacher's Role During the Home Literacy Component

1. Teachers may choose different ways to gather books back from children each week:

    - Teachers can place a box in the classroom where children can return books and label it Making Friends.

    - Teachers can tell children to put returned books in their cubbies so the books can be collected at the end of the day.

    - Teachers can ask children to place books on their desk or choose any other way that works for them.

2. A parent and child reading record can be sent home each week so teachers have a record of which children completed the activity and which children may need a little more time to complete it. Blank parent and child reading records in English and Spanish are available in Appendixes 4.6 and 4.7. When children return books, gather all parent and child reading records and organize them so they are ready for the following week's dissemination. Remind children who have not returned books that they need to bring them back.

3. It is important to remember that even though children may not bring books back, they can still choose new books during the following week so that they are still able to participate in the weekly home literacy activity. In this case, you should send reminders home that books need to be returned.

4. Send home notes that enable family members to address issues that might arise:

   • For instance, if the book's character has communication difficulties, you could send this note: "Should your child wonder how they might communicate with someone who is deaf, explain that some people communicate with their hands and fingers. Use the sign language card and try out some sign language with your child."

   • Stress that the home literacy component is not a reading assignment. Children are not expected to read the books. Rather, a family member is expected to read the book to each child and lead a discussion. If children can read, they can be encouraged to do so, but it should not be viewed as a reading assignment.

Teacher's Role After the Home Literacy Component

1. Remind children that they need to return their books, and send reminder notes to families. As previously mentioned, even though children may not bring books back, they can still choose new books during the following week.

2. Engage in conversations with families about their home book reading experiences. Answer questions and address concerns family members may have, and use natural opportunities (e.g., drop-off, pick-up, family conferences) to talk about book reading at home. Be sensitive and respectful to individual families' circumstances.

3. Engage in conversations with students about their home book reading experiences. For example, during circle time, recess, or any other activity, children may share information about book reading at home. Be responsive to children's comments, and encourage them to continue to read.

Universal Design for Learning for the Home Literacy Component

UDL Tips: Home Communication and Books

1. To help address the needs of all of the families represented in a classroom, make sure home communication informational materials or forms (e.g., letters, bookmarks, parent and child reading records) are available in the languages that are spoken in children's homes.

2. Offer audiotaped books for children who are auditory learners.

3. Provide translated books as needed.

4. Provide books online as needed.

UDL Tips: Reading and Listening to Books

Remind family members that they can use the books to meet the individual needs of their children by engaging them in different ways during the home literacy component. For example, some children may do the following:

- Read along with the story

- Tell family members the story in their own words

- Listen to the book on tape or in another language

- Participate by assisting in turning pages while a family member paraphrases (shortens) the story

UDL Tips: Responding to Guided Discussions

Remind family members that they can encourage children to express themselves in many different ways while engaging in conversations about the books. For example, some children may do the following:

- Nod or point to pictures or words in the book

- Use sign language or another primary language spoken at home

- Act out what is happening in the book

- Draw a picture of a scene from the book

- Record themselves answering questions from the book

Sometimes it takes a little time to plan how to apply UDL strategies for a home literacy activity. Examples of ways to apply UDL for this component of the program are provided in Figure 4.10, which can be used as a tool for thinking of other ideas that match the unique needs of students in a class. And of course, discussing this with family members would be an excellent way of sharing effective individualized strategies.

Scheduling the Home Literacy Component

If implementing the Making Friends program three times a week, we recommend that approximately 10 minutes be allocated on the third day of each week to enable children to select a book to take home.

LOOKING BACK, LOOKING AHEAD

This chapter introduced the three components of the Making Friends program and provided guidelines for setting up each of these components, suggestions for applying universal design for learning to meet the needs of individual children, recommendations for optimal implementation, and criteria for choosing books and materials. The chapter also provided specific ideas to help teachers understand their role before, during, and after each component to ensure purposeful planning and reflective practice.

UDL ⟶	Multiple means of representation	Multiple means of engagement	Multiple means of action and expression
Activity ⟶	Use various *formats/structures* within instructional and learning activities with differences in *task complexity and/or expectations* in response to different ability levels and *different ways children learn and communicate.*	Use multiple means to *motivate* children; *obtain and maintain attention* in response to different learning styles and challenges, interests, and preferences.	Plan for *variety in response modes to demonstrate skills* in response to different ability levels, reflecting different ways in which individuals organize and express skill/knowledge.
Home communications and books	• Provide books that depict various races, genders, and abilities. • Provide parent handouts that are easy to understand and free of educational jargon.	• Provide something for materials to be transported in, such as a clearly labeled bag, that helps children know which bag is theirs and that it has a special purpose. • Provide reinforcement for returning books and materials.	• Allow for multiple ways for parents to provide feedback on the process, such as written notes, e-mails, online surveys, and phone calls. • Have students or their parents check off, circle, initial, or write comments to demonstrate that they participated in the reading.
Reading and listening to stories	• Present stories with spoken word, sign language, or in movie format. • Provide parents with information on obtaining books on tape or other multimedia formats.	• Encourage parents to hold books with their children. • Recommend that parents treat this activity as a *special* time for them and their children to promote participation.	• Provide parents with tips to support active listening (e.g., "Each time you hear *butterfly*, make a flying butterfly."). • Suggest that parents allow their children's listening stance to change based on their needs—some may stand, sit, or lay down as they are listening.
Responding to guided discussions	• Provide parents with specific questions of varying levels of difficulty. • If needed, assist parents in noting which questions may require higher level thinking.	• Some responses can be motor movements; other responses may be verbal. • Suggest that parents ask questions when children appear to be losing focus.	• Provide parents with materials used in school, such as communication boards, PECS, or sign language information. • Recommend that parents include some choral responses (done together while reading), such as clapping, hand signals, or sign language.

Figure 4.10. Applying universal design for learning to the home literacy component.

To help ensure successful implementation of the program, you should familiarize yourself with the rest of the chapters in this book. Learning about attitude development and engaging in the reflective exercises will provide you with helpful insights about the philosophy of the program and strengthen your overall understanding of the Making Friends program. As you begin thinking about implementing the program, consider the following tips:

• Remember that practice makes perfect and that while the first few attempts to implement Making Friends may seem challenging, things will get better. If an attempt to implement a component of the program does not go that well, do not give up.

• While planning for activities, be mindful and adjust techniques to fit the unique needs of the classroom and students. What may work for some students may not work for others. Be open-minded and willing to consider alternative options to address the diverse needs of the children and families served.

- There are no rigid rules related to the implementation of the program. Make this experience meaningful for students and their families.

- Collaborate with teaching assistants, class volunteers, student teachers, related service personnel, and family members to solve issues that arise at any point in time. Teamwork can make a difference.

- Share experiences regarding program implementation with colleagues, including successes and challenges. Colleagues may help point out a new perspective or way of thinking that you had not considered before.

- Invite a colleague to come to the classroom and provide informal feedback about activities that you implemented, related to any component of the program. You can use colleagues' feedback to make changes and adapt teaching practices.

Book Selection Criteria

Diversity area	Checklist
Disability	____ The story and illustrations respectfully depict people with disabilities while not promoting stereotypes (e.g., someone who is always pitied or is always a hero).
	____ The story depicts characters with disabilities in various roles, balancing leadership roles and supporting roles of characters with and without disabilities.
	____ Characters with disabilities are portrayed realistically, having similar experiences as people without disabilities.
	____ The story uses current terminology and person-first language (e.g., "a child with Down syndrome" versus "a Down syndrome child"), avoiding offensive terms such as "slow" or "suffering from" when speaking about an individual with a disability or the disability itself.
	____ The story was written relatively recently or can be adapted when read aloud to reflect more current language or knowledge (e.g., "an autistic child" can be adapted to "a child with autism").
	____ The story was written and illustrated by individuals with knowledge of people with disabilities.
Race/ethnicity	____ The story and illustrations respectfully depict people as complex human beings rather than promoting stereotypes.
	____ Characters represent people from a variety of cultural/ethnic groups, age ranges, sizes, and abilities.
	____ The story has a balance of different people (e.g., people of color and females) in leadership or nontraditional roles.
	____ The images and information provided offer genuine insights into the lives of the characters in the story without negative value judgments about different or dominant racial or ethnic groups.
	____ The content of the story relates to children's experiences and promotes positive social and self-identities.
	____ The story was written and illustrated by individuals from a range of racial/ethnic groups and personal experiences.
	____ The story uses respectful terminology and refrains from use of historically offensive terminology such as "savage" or "primitive."
	____ The story reflects the current reality of a multicultural society.
	____ The classroom book collection depicts diversity among people within a specific racial/ethnic group.

Language	_____ The story and illustrations respectfully depict people of linguistically diverse groups as complex human beings rather than promoting stereotypes.
	_____ The abilities and strengths of people from linguistically diverse backgrounds, not their languages, are emphasized.
	_____ The story and illustrations provide authentic representations of people who use diverse communication forms.
	_____ The reading level and the vocabulary are appropriate for the target audience.
	_____ If the book is translated, the translation is accurate and includes clear, simple explanations of technical terms.
	_____ The story was written and illustrated by individuals with knowledge of people who use the language(s) portrayed in the story.
Family structure	_____ The story and illustrations respectfully depict people as complex human beings rather than promoting stereotypes.
	_____ The story depicts various family structures (e.g., single parents, extended family, adopted and foster children, stepparents, same-sex parents, family members who are incarcerated).
	_____ A variety of common life experiences are depicted.
	_____ The story depicts families without negative value judgments about diverse family structures.
	_____ The characters are described by their behaviors, beliefs, and values rather than through negative descriptors or a deficit-oriented lens (e.g., "He was adopted and has a forever family, just like you" versus "He has no family").
	_____ The book depicts a variety of traditions, clothing, foods, eating habits, and activities.
	_____ The story was written and illustrated by individuals with knowledge of various family structures.

Bookmark Discussion Guide

Title: _____

Author: _____

Aspect of diversity: _____

Content of the Story (select one or two questions, if time allows)

- _____
- _____
- _____
  _____
  _____
  _____
  _____

Explanation of Diversity or Related Vocabulary

- _____
  _____
  _____
  _____
  _____
  _____

Similarities to Highlight

- How is _____ in the story like you?
  _____
  _____
  _____
  _____
  _____
  _____

Equipment, Materials, or Tools Related to Story Content

- _____
  _____
  _____
  _____
  _____
  _____

Discussion Prompts

- Talk about what it might be like to play with a friend who _____.
  _____
  _____
  _____
  _____
  _____

Thanks for taking 15 minutes to read and talk about this book with me!

Toys and Materials Selection Criteria

Use toys and materials that . . .

____ allow some manipulation but are not so intricate as to require the child's whole attention.

____ depict a variety of abilities, races/ethnicities, languages, and family structures.

____ include an element of sociodramatic play or items that might be adapted for sociodramatic play (i.e., toys and materials with high social value that are easy to make up stories with, such as grocery store, restaurant, or cooking and eating toys).

____ encourage children to seek information from each other.

____ may require children to seek the help of others in playing or operating (either physical assistance or verbal instructions).

____ have a number of parts, but not so many parts that the majority of the time will be spent examining all of the pieces. A small number of parts also will promote sharing among students.

____ maintain the students' attention for the entire length of the cooperative play activity.

____ promote mutual use by two or more students as opposed to solitary play.

____ are the appropriate size for children with different abilities.

Home Communication Letter

Date: _____

Dear parents and guardians,

We are very excited to introduce the Making Friends program in our classroom! This classwide program is designed to celebrate human diversity and to increase understanding and acceptance of differences. Over the next several weeks, we will focus on diversity topics, such as people with disabilities, people from diverse racial and ethnic backgrounds, people who use different languages to communicate, and people from unique family structures.

The Making Friends program has three components: school literacy, cooperative learning, and home literacy. The first two components take place in school (we encourage you to talk with your child about these), while the final component takes place in the home environment.

Here is what you need to know:

It's very simple! Each week, your child will bring home a carefully selected book that includes diverse characters and a discussion guide. Together, you and your child will read the book and talk about it. Here are a few tips for reading with your child:

- Sit so you are both comfortable and can see the pages easily.
- Let your child hold the book and turn the pages.
- Look at the book's cover and make a prediction about the content of the story.
- Take a "tour of the book" before reading by looking at the pictures and talking about them.
- As you read the book, engage in conversation with your child about what he or she sees in the pictures and hears in the storyline. Point out similarities between the book's characters and your child.
- After reading the book together, engage your child in a conversation about the story using the bookmark discussion guide.

And that's it! Talking about diversity can provide a new and exciting opportunity to celebrate our shared human diversity. The time you spend engaging with your child helps build a supportive and inclusive classroom environment for all students. Thank you for helping us meet this goal. Please let me know if you have any questions, suggestions, or comments. I look forward to working with you and your child on the Making Friends program. Happy reading!

Sincerely,

_____

Home Communication Letter in Spanish

Fecha: _____

Estimados padres y tutores,

¡Estamos muy emocionados de presentar el programa *Haciendo Amigos* en nuestro salón de clases! Este programa para toda la clase está diseñado para celebrar la diversidad humana y aumentar la comprensión y la aceptación de las diferencias entre personas. Durante las próximas semanas, nos centraremos en temas de la diversidad como las personas con discapacidad, las personas de diversos orígenes raciales y étnicos, las personas que utilizan diferentes lenguas para comunicarse y las personas de las estructuras familiares únicas.

El programa *Haciendo Amigos* tiene tres componentes: alfabetización escolar, aprendizaje cooperativo y alfabetización en el hogar. Los primeros dos componentes serán actualizados en la escuela (les pedimos que hablen con su hijo o hija sobre estos componentes), mientras que el ultimo componente será actualizado en el hogar.

Esto es lo que tienen que saber:

¡Es muy fácil! Cada semana, su hijo llevará a casa uno de los libros, que fueron cuidadosamente elegidos y que incluyen personajes diversos, y una guía de discusión. Juntos, usted y su hijo o hija leerán el libro y hablarán juntos sobre el libro Aquí hay algunos consejos para leer con su hijo o hija:

- Siéntense para que ambos estén cómodos y puedan ver las páginas fácilmente.
- Deje que su niño sostenga el libro y pase las páginas.
- Miren la portada del libro y hagan una predicción sobre el contenido de la historia.
- Tomen un "tour del libro" antes de leer, mirando las fotos y hablando sobre ellas.
- Después de leer el libro juntos, participen en una conversación acerca de la historia, utilizando la guía para discusión en el marcapáginas.

¡Y eso es todo! Hablando de diversidad puede proveer una nueva y emocionante oportunidad de celebrar nuestra diversidad humana compartida. El tiempo que usted pasa con su hijo o hija ayuda a crear un ambiente inclusivo y apoyador para todos los estudiantes en la clase. Gracias por ayudarnos a alcanzar esta meta. Por favor déjeme saber si tiene alguna pregunta, sugerencia, o comentario. Espero con interés trabajar con usted y su hijo o hija en el programa *Haciendo Amigos*. ¡Diviértanse leyendo!

Atentamente,

_____

Parent and Child Reading Record

Child's name: _____   Teacher's name: _____

Parent and Child Reading Record

Dear parent or guardian,

This form will enable us to keep up with the home reading component of the Making Friends program. Please keep this form in your child's Ziplock bag until the program is complete.

All the stories that your child chooses to bring home will be listed below across the 6-week program. When you have read and discussed each story with your child, place your initials in the middle column. Record any comments you have about the story in the last column. Return the book and this record at the beginning of every week.

Thank you!

	Story title	Parent initials	Comments
Week 1			
Week 2			
Week 3			
Week 4			
Week 5			
Week 6			

Parent and Child Reading Record in Spanish

Nombre del niño/a: _____ Nombre del maestro: _____

Registro de Lectura de Padre e Hijo

Estimado padre o tutor,

Este formulario nos permitirá estar al día con el componente de lectura en el hogar del programa *Haciendo Amigos*. Por favor, mantenga este formulario en la bolsa de plástico de su hijo/a hasta que el programa se haya completado.

   Todas las historias que su hijo elija para llevar a casa se enumerarán a continuación a través del programa de seis semanas. Cuando haya leído y discutido cada historia con su hijo, coloque sus iniciales en la columna central. Escriba cualquier comentario que tenga acerca de la historia en la última columna. Entregue el libro y este registro al comienzo de cada semana.

¡Gracias!

	Título de la historia	Iniciales del padre	Comentarios
Semana 1			
Semana 2			
Semana 3			
Semana 4			
Semana 5			
Semana 6			

CHAPTER 5

Resources for the School and Home Environments

TOOLBOX

Appendix 5.1. Books About Diversity: A List of Recommendations for Classroom Use

Appendix 5.2. Web Resources for Book Collections Representing Diversity

Appendix 5.3. Web Resources for Toys and Materials Depicting Children from Diverse Backgrounds

Appendix 5.4. Web Resources for Toys and Materials Depicting Diverse Communication

Appendix 5.5. Web Resources for Classroom Materials Reflecting Diversity or Differences

---

IMPORTANCE OF A RESOURCE-RICH ENVIRONMENT

As explained in the previous chapters, promoting acceptance of and friendships with others is dependent on the influences from *indirect experiences* (e.g., conversations, books, videos, curriculum materials, toys), *direct experiences* with people (e.g., individuals who have a disability, speak other languages, or are from diverse backgrounds), and the child's *primary social group* (family and peers). Therefore, it is important to address all of these influences.

However, one easily overlooked aspect of attitude formation is the influence of indirect experiences. Imagine a child looking around his classroom or school and not seeing any images of himself in the books, lesson materials, toys, or posters (Blaska, 2000; Hughes et al., 2006; Joshua, 2002). Imagine not hearing any conversations that reflect you, your culture, your family, or your way of life. As mentioned in earlier chapters, when this type of omission happens, it sends two strong messages: The child who is not depicted in the images might think, "I do not belong. I don't count. I am not important." The other children may have similar thoughts, such as "He is not one of us. He is not equal to us." And while teachers and families do not intend to send such messages, it may be the unintentional consequence of the lack of diversity in the materials in school and home environments. Simply put, whereas early childhood classes have become increasingly diverse and more inclusive over the last decade, there is still a lag in the presence of multicultural resources (e.g., print and visual media) that reflect the incredible diversity observed in children and families.

Michael understood that differences are not bad. He liked that Isabelle [a book character] could do many of the same things as Charlie [another character in the book].
—*Ms. Pinteris*

In a recent study of 32 inclusive kindergarten classes, teachers reported that 30 of the classes had little or no representation of individuals with disabilities in the books, curricula, and classroom materials (Ostrosky et al., 2012). This lack of images of people with disabilities is a reflection of the broader societal challenge also faced by other groups who struggle for greater representation in print and visual media. For example, young Caucasian characters represent 73% of prime-time television portrayals, African Americans represent 16%, and Latinos represent only 1% of characters (excluding all-Spanish channels such as Telemundo; Children Now, 2004). Only 3% of children's books are authored by or are about Latinos, even though 25% of all public school children are Latino (Horning, Lindgren, & Schliesman, 2013).

A focus on resource-rich and diverse curricular environments is long overdue. Intentionally providing an array of resources to reflect diversity will in turn affirm a sense of belonging for all children and set the stage for influential conversations about the rich diversity in the world. To achieve this outcome, school, community, and home environments need to be infused with a rich array of materials that inform and positively affect all children.

RESOURCES FOR MAKING FRIENDS

Several resources that reflect children and families from diverse backgrounds are included in this chapter to help facilitate the successful implementation of the Making Friends program. A book list representing each diversity area addressed in *Making Friends* is provided in Appendix 5.1; these stories contain characters with disabilities and diverse racial, ethnic, and language backgrounds as well as family structures. These books have been evaluated and meet the criteria for inclusion in the Making Friends program, thereby enabling teachers to get started easily. In addition to the book list, other resources in this chapter include the following:

- Web links for additional books related to diversity (Appendix 5.2)

- Web links for materials and toys that depict diversity (Appendix 5.3)

- Web links for materials and toys related to diverse communication modes (Appendix 5.4)

- Web links for classroom materials that reflect diversity (Appendix 5.5)

Because all three components of the Making Friends program depend on having a resource-rich environment that reflects all kinds of diversity, these links to materials will be helpful for the school literacy component, home literacy activities, and cooperative learning groups. After completing the Diversity in School Environments exercise

(Appendix 3.4), use these resources to identify materials and activities that could be added to your classroom prior to implementing the Making Friends program.

TIPS FOR SUCCESS

Ordering Materials

I am more comfortable being able to talk to the kids about disabilities.
—Mr. Shaffer

- Order materials early to avoid delays in starting the Making Friends program.

- Order materials in bulk (e.g., multiple teachers or multiple schools might join together to purchase resources), which can reduce shipping costs and may reduce the price of materials.

- Some schools support teachers in having "wish lists" when they have book fairs; these are lists that family members can use to buy extra classroom books. Add some of the books from the book lists to the "wish list."

Sharing Lists and Links

- The lists of books and links to other resources can be shared with parents and other family members so they can enhance their home environment.

- The resources can be shared with the larger school community, including other teachers, guidance counselors, and librarians.

- Limited funds for classroom materials may discourage some teachers from broadening the variety of materials available to their students. However, if schools are to meet children's social and emotional needs and Common Core Standards, then recommendations for culturally responsive classrooms, including diverse materials, should be viewed as essential. Because of this, the Making Friends program and the resources provided in this chapter should be shared with school supervisors and administrators who oversee the allocation of resources and the purchasing of materials.

- Teachers are strongly encouraged to share the Making Friends materials, such as the book and materials lists, with the community librarian to ensure that the local community provides materials and books that counter the diversity gap in children's books.

Using Lists and Links

I learned a lot from the whole project and the overall experience.
—Ms. Russo

- Teachers are encouraged to provide simple explanations about diversity. While field-testing the Making Friends program, many teachers stated that they did not know how to talk about human differences, and some were uncomfortable discussing the sensitive topic of diversity. Providing simple standard explanations for teachers (in the discussion guides) seemed to help address this issue.

- Teachers can use one or more of these books as a summer reading activity for family members and children in preparation for the Making Friends program.

- Access to materials should be an ongoing and natural part of the class and school curriculum, not just a onetime event.

- Teachers and family members alike are strongly encouraged to use the materials presented in the lists not just for entertainment purposes but rather as a means to create teachable moments about human differences through informed and sensitive discussions.

- Use the local library as a resource for borrowing books on the book lists.

- Easy access to and storage of materials is critical to ensure that they are readily available for both teachers and children.

- Teachers often know which children might work better together in small group activities This knowledge should be used when arranging cooperative learning groups, taking care to not place children who might encourage off-task behavior in the same groups.

Timothy loved practicing sign language while we read the book.
—Mr. Hasan

- It is important that children are not singled out in discussions (e.g., "This book is about a boy with autism. Alex in Ms. Eacott's class has autism."). Family members need to be assured that their children will not receive unwanted attention during class discussions. However, natural observations of human differences occur every day in classrooms and within school and community settings, so family members also need to be assured that these discussions will be handled in a positive and matter-of-fact manner (as in the previous example of Maggie).

Supporting Families

- Some family members may be reluctant about discussing human differences or are unsure of how to do so. Use the models provided in this book and the resources in the appendixes to this chapter to assist family members in discussing diversity at home.

- Remind family members that books and materials are to be shared with their children to foster conversations about diversity, as opposed to using the books for the children to demonstrate reading ability or for purely entertainment purposes without discussion.

- Should family members or teachers hear children making inaccurate comments about individuals who are different from them (e.g., "She can't talk, she's a baby."), they should provide correct information at an appropriate development level (e.g., "Maggie isn't a baby, she is 6 just like you. Just like some friends in our class are learning to tie shoes and zip up their coats while other friends already know how to do these things, Maggie is learning to talk using sign language.").

- Provide parents with simple standard explanations in the bookmark discussion guides to enable parents to talk about diversity more easily.

LOOKING FORWARD

After looking through the Making Friends manual, completing all of the reflective exercises, and evaluating classroom and school environments, it is time to begin planning the for the Making Friends program. This is an exciting moment as teachers begin this important undertaking. One parent said after participating in the program, *"Aside from learning to read, this was the most valuable new skill my child learned in this school year—to accept and befriend children with differences. Both are skills that my son will use his whole life."* Now is the time to make that kind of impact a reality for all students!

I learned that I am special!
—Eleni, 6 years old

Books About Diversity: A List of Recommendations for Home and Classroom Use

Books About Children with Disabilities

Title	Author	Date	Publisher	Description
All Kinds of Friends, Even Green!	Ellen B. Senisi	2002	Woodbine House	A boy in a wheelchair writes about his iguana that also has a physical disability.
Andy and His Yellow Frisbee	Mary Thompson	1996	Woodbine House	At school, a girl befriends a young boy who has autism.
Be Quiet, Marina!	Kristen DeBear	2014	Starbright Books	Two young girls are friends; one child has cerebral palsy and one has Down syndrome.
Don't Call Me Special: A First Look at Disability	Pat Thomas	2005	Barron's Educational Series	Children with a variety of disabilities are shown participating in everyday activities.
Friends at School	Rochelle Bunnett	2006	Starbright Books	Children with a variety of disabilities work and play together at school.
Ian's Walk	Laurie Lears	1998	Albert Whitman & Company	A young boy with autism sees things in a unique way on his walk through the park.
Let's Talk About It: Extraordinary Friends	Fred Rogers	2000	Puffin	Children with a variety of disabilities participate in friendships with their peers.
The Night Search	Kate Chamberlin	1997	Jason & Nordic Publishers	A young girl who is blind goes camping with her family.
Someone Special Just Like You	Tricia Brown	1995	Henry Holt & Co.	Children with a variety of disabilities participate in activities with their peers.
Susan Laughs	Jeanne Willis	2000	Henry Holt & Co.	A young girl with a physical disability participates in everyday activities.
We Can Do It!	Laura Dwight	2005	Starbright Books	Children with a variety of disabilities participate in everyday activities.
We'll Paint the Octopus Red	Stephanie Stuve-Bodeen	1998	Woodbine House	A girl welcomes a baby brother, who has Down syndrome.

Books About Children from Diverse Racial or Ethnic Backgrounds

Title	Author	Date	Publisher	Description
A Is for Abraham: A Jewish Family Alphabet	Richard Michelson	2008	Sleeping Bear Press	An alphabet book format is used to describe various Jewish cultures and traditions.
Amazing Grace	Mary Hoffman	1991	Dial	Grace, a young African American girl, realizes she can accomplish any goal she sets for herself.
Bigmama's	Donald Crews	1998	Greenwillow Books	An African American man remembers his boyhood travels to visit "Bigmama" in Florida.
Black Is Brown Is Tan	Arnold Adoff	1973	Harper Collins	This poetic story is about the everyday activities within a mixed-race family.
Honey, I Love, and Other Poems	Eloise Greenfield	1986	Harper Collins	This collection of poems is written from the perspective of an African American girl.

Title	Author	Date	Publisher	Description
Jingle Dancer	Cynthia Leitich Smith	2000	Harper Collins	A young Native American girl wants to learn to dance like her grandmother.
Ling and Ting: Not Exactly the Same!	Grace Lin	2011	LB Kids	Ling and Ting are Chinese American twin sisters who like to do things together, but not always in the same way.
Morning on the Lake	Jan Bourdeau Waboose	1997	Kids Can Press	A Native American boy and his grandfather spend a day together in the wilderness.
My Mother's Sari	Sandhya Rao	2009	NorthSouth	A girl in an Indian family is fascinated by her mother's sari.
One World, One Day	Barbara Kerley	2009	National Geographic Society	This book uses photographs and simple language to show how children from various cultures around the world share common activities.
Shades of Black: A Celebration of Our Children	Sandra L. Pinkney	2000	Scholastic	Photographs and poetic language are used to celebrate African American children.
Uncle Peter's Amazing Chinese Wedding	Lenore Look	2006	Atheneum Books	A young girl learns about traditional Chinese ceremonies when she participates in her uncle's wedding.

Books About Children Who Use Diverse Languages

Title	Author	Date	Publisher	Description
Can You Hear a Rainbow?	Jamee Riggio Heelan	2002	Peachtree Pub Ltd	Chris, who is deaf, uses sign language and lip reading to communicate with family and friends.
Cookie	Linda Kneeland	1999	Jason & Nordic Publishers	Molly, who is deaf, uses sign language to communicate.
The Dancer	Fred Burstein	1993	Simon & Schuster	A young girl and her father walk through their neighborhood together. The narrative highlights their adventures in English, Spanish, and Japanese.
The Deaf Musicians	Pete Seeger Paul Jacobs	2006	Putnam Juvenile	Deaf musicians, who use sign language to communicate, perform in the city.
Going Home, Coming Home / Ve Nha Tham Que Huong	Truong Tran	2003	Children's Book Press	A girl visits her grandmother in Vietnam; the grandmother introduces her to the Vietnamese language.
Margaret and Margarita / Margarita y Margaret	Lynn Reiser	1996	Greenwillow Books	Two young girls meet in the park and play together. One girl speaks Spanish and one speaks English.
Moses Goes to a Concert	Isaac Millman	2002	Square Fish	Moses, who is deaf and uses sign language to communicate, enjoys a concert with his classmates.
My Way / A mi manera	Lynn Reiser	2007	Harper Collins	Two girls describe activities in their everyday lives, one using English and one using Spanish.

Title	Author	Date	Publisher	Description
The Name Jar	Yangsook Choi	2003	Dragonfly Books	A young Korean girl, new to America, considers choosing an American name. Eventually she embraces her name in Korean.
One Green Apple	Eve Bunting	2006	Clarion Books	A young Muslim girl, who is an English language learner, connects with classmates on a trip to the apple orchard.
Sarah's Surprise	Nan Holcomb	1990	Jason & Nordic Publishers	A young girl uses an augmentative/ alternative communication (AAC) device to sing "Happy Birthday" to her mother.
Walk with Grandpa / Un paseo con el abuelo	Sharon Solomon	2009	Raven Tree Press	On a walk through the woods, a young girl and her grandfather play a word game in English and Spanish.

Books About Children with Diverse Family Structures

Title	Author	Date	Publisher	Description
Bringing Home Asha	Uma Krishnaswami	2006	Lee & Low Books	A young Hindu boy is excited to learn that his family will be adopting a baby girl from India.
A Chair for My Mother	Vera B. Williams	2007	Greenwillow Books	A family who experiences poverty after losing their belongings in a fire saves coins to buy a new chair.
The Day We Met You	Phoebe Koehler	1997	Aladdin	This book tells the story of one family's joyful experience with open adoption.
The Family Book	Todd Parr	2010	Little Brown Books	This picture book affirms a variety of family structures.
Felicia's Favorite Story	Leslea Newman	2002	Two Lives Pub	This story is about a girl with two moms who loves to hear the story of her adoption.
Let's Talk About It: Stepfamilies	Fred Rogers	2001	Puffin	Using photographs, this book highlights some of the joys and struggles that may come with joining a stepfamily.
Maybe Days: A Book for Children in Foster Care	Jennifer Wilgocki	2002	American Psychological Association	This book addresses many of the questions and concerns that children in foster care may have.
The Night Dad Went to Jail	Melissa Higgins	2011	Picture Window Books	Sketch has a father who is incarcerated. The adults in Sketch's life help him understand his emotions about this experience.
Sometimes Its Grandmas and Grandpas (Not Mommies and Daddies)	Gayle Byrne	2009	Abbeville Kids	This story is about a happy young girl who is raised by her grandparents.
A Tale of Two Daddies	Vanita Oelschlager	2010	Vanita Books	A girl tells a classmate about her life with two dads.
Totally Uncool	Janice Levy	2001	Carolrhoda Books	A girl in a single-parent family learns to accept her father's girlfriend.
We All Have Different Families	Melissa Higgins	2012	Capstone Press	This picture book describes many family structures, including grandparents, foster families, and single-parent families.

Web Resources for Book Collections Representing Diversity

Children's Books to Support Antibias Education

http://www.childpeacebooks.org/cpb/Protect/antiBias.php

This site provides a list of children's books selected by Julie Olsen Edwards, coauthor of the *Anti-Bias Education for Young Children and Ourselves*. It offers suggestions for culture and language, racial identity, gender roles, economic class, abilities and disabilities, family structure, holidays, activism, and infant/toddler books.

Colorin Colorado—Books for Kids

http://www.colorincolorado.org/read/forkids/

This site provides a variety of book lists. Relevant topics related to diversity include English language learner (ELL) stories, immigrant stories, books in two languages, holidays and festivals, adoption stories, grandparent stories, reading with mom/dad, family and cultural traditions, African stories, American Indian heritage, Asian Pacific American heritage, African American history, and Hispanic heritage.

Children's Books About Disabilities

https://www.teachervision.com/learning-disabilities/reading/5316.html

This site provides a comprehensive list of children's books related to having a disability.

Fifty Multicultural Books Every Child Should Know

http://ccbc.education.wisc.edu/books/detailListBooks.asp?idBookLists=42

This list offers ideas for enriching a classroom's library of multicultural books. It was compiled by the Cooperative Children's Book Center at the University of Wisconsin–Madison.

Selecting Culturally Appropriate Children's Books in Languages Other than English

http://eclkc.ohs.acf.hhs.gov/hslc/tta-system/cultural-linguistic/fcp/docs/ncclr-qguide-select-cultural-childrens-books-non -english.pdf

Published by the National Center on Cultural and Linguistic Responsiveness, this guide helps teachers find, select, evaluate, and use books in languages other than English to support language and literacy development.

Welcoming Family Diversity in the Classroom

http://www.educationworld.com/a_curr/welcoming-diverse-family-structures.shtml

This resource by Education World offers suggestions, including books, for affirming diversity of family structure in the classroom.

Teaching for Change

http://www.tfcbooks.org/best-recommended/booklist

This resource offers suggestions for enriching school and home libraries with children's books that reflect multicultural authors and stories.

Web Resources for Toys and Materials
Depicting Children from Diverse Backgrounds

Diversity area	Web site	Description
Disabilities	Lakeshore Block Play People with Differing Abilities http://www.lakeshorelearning.com	Figurines of people with diverse abilities (e.g., a boy using a wheelchair, a woman with a guide dog, a girl with a walker) and adaptive equipment
	Marvel Education Company Pretend and Play™ Friends with Diverse Abilities Set http://www.kaplantoys.com	
	Adaptive Equipment for Dolls with Special Needs—Complete Set http://www.lakeshorelearning.com	
	Differing Abilities Puzzle Set http://www.lakeshorelearning.com	Puzzles that portray people with disabilities participating in various daily activities (e.g., a boy with leg braces planting a garden, a boy with a walker playing musical instruments with classmates)
	Preschool Friends Together Poster http://www.kaplantoys.com	Posters that show children with diverse abilities playing and learning together
Race/ethnicity	Kids Around the World Block Play People http://www.lakeshorelearning.com	Figures and puppets of people with a range of skin tones and hair colors
	Lego Duplo World People Set http://www.legoeducation.us	
	Kids Around the World Finger Puppets http://www.orientaltrading.com	
	JC Toys Realistic Ethnic Baby Dolls http://www.jctoys.com	Baby dolls with a range of skin tones and hair colors
	Flags of All Nations Line-of-Flags http://www.orientaltrading.com	Flags of other nations
	Traditional Children's Games http://www.topics-mag.com/edition11/games-section.htm	Traditional children's games from around the world
	Sushi Slicing Play Set	Toy food, cookware, and utensils of other cultures (e.g., curry, sushi, burritos, woks, chopsticks)
	Stir Fry Slicing Play Set	
	Taco and Burrito Play Set http://www.melissaanddoug.com	
	Teaching World Cultures http://www.learning.org/lp/pages/6390	Clothing from other cultures (e.g., flamenco dresses, kimonos)
	Culture Connect: Experience Cultures of the World Through the Haffenreffer Museum of Anthropology http://www.brown.edu/Facilities/Haffenreffer/documents/CultureConnectteacherpacketfinal.pdf	
	Musical Instruments from Around the World http://www.youtube.com/watch?v=XBs9UCetgog	Musical instruments from other cultures (e.g., ukulele, djembe)
	Foreign Banknotes from Around the World and Foreign Coins Assortment http://www.amazon.com	Coins and money from different countries

Diversity area	Web site	Description
Language	International Foods http://www.guidecraft.com	Ethnic food boxes with print in different languages for dramatic play
	Laugh and Learn™ Learning Table http://www.fisher-price.com	Toys that make sounds in languages other than English (e.g., "yellow" and "amarillo" when the yellow button is pressed)
	Numeros Bingo Game: Numbers in Spanish http://www.trendenterprises.com	Picture- and word-matching games with different languages (e.g., matching number "2" and the word "dos")
	Colores y Formas Bingo Game: Colors and Shapes in Spanish http://www.trendenterprises.com	
	Hello to All the Children of the World http://www.youtube.com/watch?v=GpTR1wF4M6k	Songs that teach different languages
	Wee Sing Around the World http://www.weesing.com	Simple children's songs and rhymes in multiple languages
	Multicultural Music Resources http://www.teachervision.com/Multiculturalism/resource/8388.html	
	Mama Lisa's World International Music and Culture http://www.mamalisa.com	
Family structure	Pottery Barn Kids Dollhouses and Families http://www.potterybarnkids.com	Various types of toy homes or pictures of homes (e.g., house, apartment, condo, townhouse, farm house)
	City Family, Farm Family, Geometrics House, All Season House, Happy Villa http://www.hapetoys.com	
	Marvel Education Company Pretend and Play™ Family http://www.kaplantoys.com	Figurines of people with various ages, genders, and ethnicities
	Happy Family http://www.hapetoys.com	
	Families Poster Pack http://www.lakeshorelearning.com	Pictures of diverse family structures to post in the play area (e.g., grandparents with children, parents with an adopted child, single mother and children, two fathers with a child)
	The ART of Family Building http://www.mljadoptions.com/wp-content/uploads/converted/userfiles/file/PDFs/Teachers%20Guide.pdf	Resources for discussing adoption (including alternatives to the family-tree assignment)
	Welcoming Schools: A Project of the Human Rights Campaign Foundation http://www.welcomingschools.org	Resources for discussing lesbian, gay, bisexual, and transgender (LGBT) topics
	Little Children, Big Challenges: Incarceration http://www.sesamestreet.org/Parents/topicsandactivities/toolkits/Incarceration	Tool kits for children who have a family member who is incarcerated

Web Resources for Toys and Materials Depicting Diverse Communication

Way of communication	Web site	Description
Sign language	Differing Abilities Poster Pack http://www.lakeshorelearning.com	Posters that portray children communicating in various ways (e.g., a girl reading in braille, a mother and a child using sign language)
	Sign Language ABC-123 Poster http://www.maxiaids.com	Sign language posters
	Sign Language Blocks http://www.unclegoose.com	Sign language blocks
	Sign Language Bingo http://www.maxiaids.com	Sign language board games
	Match-Up Puzzles: First Signs http://www.harriscomm.com	Sign language matching games
	American Sign Language Dictionary http://www.start-american-sign-language.com/american-sign-language-dictionary.html	Useful for labeling classroom areas and materials with sign language
Braille	Board Games with Braille Marks http://www.enablemart.com http://www.braillebookstore.com	Board games with braille marks (e.g., Bingo, Scrabble, Monopoly)
	Wooden Blocks with Braille Letters http://www.unclegoose.com	Wooden blocks with braille letters
	Dice and Dominoes with Braille Letters, Braille Books, Audio Books http://www.braillebookstore.com	Dice and dominoes with braille letters, braille books, audio books
	Braille Learning Doll http://www.assistivetech.net	Braille learning doll
	Braille Contraction Dictionary http://www.brl.org/refdesk/Conlookup.html	Useful for labeling classroom areas and materials in braille
Picture exchange communication system (PECS)	Pyramid Educational Consultants http://www.pecsusa.com	Useful for creating class schedules and routines using PECS symbols
	Boardmaker™ Picture Symbols http://www.mayer-johnson.com	Useful for creating class rules (e.g., no talking, hands to yourself) using PECS symbols
	Special Education Technology British Columbia http://www.setbc.org/pictureset	Useful for creating storybooks and flashcards with PECS symbols

Way of communication	Web site	Description
Languages other than English	Bilingual Reminder Poster Set http://www.carsondellosa.com	Useful for writing rules, directions, and reminders in multiple languages
	Print-Rich Classroom Labels: Spanish Bulletin Board Set http://www.carsondellosa.com	Bulletin board in multiple languages
	Las Manzanas Rojas Motivational Stickers http://www.carsondellosa.com	Reward stickers in Spanish (e.g., Bravo! Bien Hecho!)
	Uncle Goose Blocks in 21 Different Languages http://www.unclegoose.com	Wooden blocks in multiple languages
	Chinese and English Nursery Rhymes: Share and Sing in Two Languages (Book and Audio CD) http://books.simonandschuster.com/Chinese-and-English-Nursery-Rhymes/Faye-Lynn-Wu/9780804840941	Books and audio books in multiple languages
	Free Online Dictionaries in Multiple Languages http://www.wordreference.com	Useful for labeling classroom areas and materials in multiple languages (e.g., "library" and "*bibliotek*")

Web Resources for Classroom Materials Reflecting Diversity or Differences

Diversity area	Web site	Description
General	Teaching Tolerance http://www.tolerance.org/	This web site provides thought-provoking news, conversations, and support for those who care about diversity, equal opportunity, and respect for differences in schools. It includes a free magazine for educators, professional development resources, and classroom resources.
	Teaching for Change http://www.teachingforchange.org/	This web site encourages teachers and students to rethink the world inside and outside their classrooms; build a more equitable, multicultural society; and become active global citizens.
Disability	Toy Box Tools http://toyboxtools.hasbro.com/ Toy Guide for Differently Abled Kids http://www.toysrus.com/shop/index.jsp?categoryId=3261680	These two web sites have tools to encourage development during playtime. They also include a list of toys and suggestions for how to use them with children who have disabilities or developmental delays.
	Special Needs Resource Center https://www.fatbraintoys.com/special_needs/	This web site categorizes toys according to how they have been used successfully by children with various disabilities (e.g., toys that meet the needs of children with quadriplegia).
	Including Children with Special Needs: Are You and Your Program Ready? https://www.naeyc.org/files/yc/file/200903/BTJWatson.pdf	This article provides teachers with a checklist to help them evaluate how various program elements (e.g., home–school communication, curriculum, assessment) are meeting the needs of children with disabilities. The checklist also helps programs evaluate their readiness to accommodate children with a variety of disabilities (e.g., physical disabilities, hearing or vision impairments, sensory integration concerns).
Race/ethnicity	Multicultural Education Pavilion http://www.edchange.org/multicultural/index.html	This web site provides resources related to diversity, equity, and social justice education and includes teacher resources, awareness activities, and steps for multicultural curriculum reform.
	The National Center for Culturally Responsive Educational Systems http://www.nccrest.org/	This initiative supports state and local school systems to assure high-quality and culturally responsive education for all students. Teachers can gain access to a variety of publications, including practitioner briefs, tools for quality improvement, DVDs, and state profiles addressing disproportionality in special education.
	International Pen Friends http://usa.ipfpenfriends.com/	This pen-pal club establishes connections between individuals around the world. Teachers can use this site to arrange pen pals for their class.
Language	Teaching Diverse Learners http://www.brown.edu/academics/education-alliance/teaching-diverse-learners/	This web site provides access to resources for teacher candidates and practicing teachers who want to improve their practice in working with English language learners (ELLs).
	The Teaching Channel https://www.teachingchannel.org/videos/multilingual-classroom-teaching	The teaching channel is an online community "where teachers can watch, share, and learn diverse techniques to help every student grow." This link is to one of several videos related to teaching in a multilingual classroom.
	¡Colorin Colorado! http://www.colorincolorado.org/	This bilingual site for families and educators of ELLs provides a variety of resources, including ELL issues in the news, research and policy reports, and teaching tools.

Diversity area	Web site	Description
Language	International Children's Digital Library http://en.childrenslibrary.org/	This digital library has outstanding children's books from around the world. Books represent a variety of languages and cultures.
	Language Castle http://www.languagecastle.com	This web site, blog, and book (*Many Languages, One Classroom: Teaching Dual and English Language Learners*) offer suggestions for supporting children who are learning English.
	National Head Start Office Early Childhood Learning and Knowledge Center (ECLKC): National Center on Cultural and Linguistic Responsiveness http://eclkc.ohs.acf.hhs.gov/hslc	This web site has a variety of tools, including the downloadable "Program Preparedness Checklist: Serving Dual Language Learners and Their Families." It also offers information on appropriate assessment, planning, and teaching children who are learning English.
Family structure	LGBT Inclusive Curriculum Guide for Educators http://glsen.org/educate/resources/creating-lgbt-inclusive-lessons	This curriculum guide offers best practices, planning tips, connections to Common Core Standards, and guided reflection—all in relation to LGBT inclusiveness.
	Welcoming Schools http://www.welcomingschools.org/	This web site offers professional development tools; lessons aligned with the Common Core State Standards; and other resources for embracing family diversity, avoiding gender stereotyping and affirming gender, and ending bullying and name calling.
	Welcoming Family Diversity in the Classroom http://www.educationworld.com/a_curr/welcoming-diverse-family-structures.shtml	This article in *Education World* offers five ways that educators can celebrate diversity of family structure.
	Little Children, Big Challenges: Incarceration http://www.sesamestreet.org/parents/topicsandactivities/toolkits/incarceration	This tool kit for parents and providers offers resources to support a child through a parent's incarceration.
	Teacher's Guide to Adoption http://www.familyhelper.net/ad/adteach.html	This resource includes several modules to help teachers address the issue of adoption. A variety of family structures (e.g., same-sex parents, foster parents) are discussed as well.
	Adoptive Families https://www.adoptivefamilies.com	This web site, associated with the national magazine *Adoptive Families*, includes teaching resources for families wishing to share their adoption experience with their child's school.
	Children Who Live in "Out-of-Home" Care or Foster Care http://www.kidshelp.com.au/kids/information/hot-topics/foster-care.php	This resource by Kids Helpline addresses aspects of foster care (e.g., siblings, case workers, seeing mom and dad) in a simple and matter-of-fact way, presented at a child's level.
	Helping Children Adjust to Divorce: A Guide for Teachers http://extension.missouri.edu/publications/DisplayPub.aspx?P=GH6611	This guide by the University of Missouri provides advice for teachers about helping students in their class adjust to divorce.
	Supporting Children of Divorce: Guidelines for Caregivers http://www.ianrpubs.unl.edu/pages/publicationD.jsp?publicationId=272	This guide by the University of Nebraska–Lincoln gives caregivers advice on how to help children deal with their emotions during a difficult time.

References

Aboud, F., Mendelson, M., & Purdy, K. (2003). Cross-race peer relations and friendship quality. *International Journal of Behavioral Development, 27*(2), 165–173.

Ajzen, I. (1988). *Attitudes, personality, and behavior.* Chicago, IL: Dorsey.

Ajzen, I. (2001). Nature and operation of attitudes. *Annual Review of Psychology, 52*(1), 27–58.

Allport, G.W. (1935). Attitudes. In C. Murchison (Ed.), *Handbook of social psychology* (pp. 798–844). Worcester, MA: Clark University Press.

Baker, C., & Jones, S. (1989). Attitudes to languages. In C. Baker & S. Jones (Eds.), *Encyclopedia of bilingualism and bilingual education* (pp. 174–180). Clevedon, UK: Multilingual Matters Ltd.

Barnes, C. (1992). *Disabling imagery and the media: An exploration of the principles for media representations of disabled people.* Krumlin, UK: British Council of Organizations of Disabled People and Ryburn Publishing Limited.

Beckman, P.J., & Kohl, F.L. (1984). The effects of social and isolate toys on the interactions and play of integrated and nonintegrated groups of preschoolers. *Education and Training of the Mentally Retarded, 12,* 169–174.

Blaska, J.K. (2000). Literacy richness in early childhood environments. *Your Link,* Summer, p. 7.

Bliss, S.K., & Harris, M.B. (1998). Experiences of gay and lesbian teachers and parents with coming out in school settings. *Journal of Gay and Lesbian Social Sciences, 8*(2), 174–180.

Bricker, D. (1995). The challenge of inclusion. *Journal of Early Intervention, 19,* 179–194.

Brown, W.H., Odom, S.L., & Conroy, M.A. (2001). An intervention hierarchy for promoting preschool children's peer interactions in natural environments. *Topics in Early Childhood Special Education, 21,* 90–134.

Castelli, L., Zogmaister, C., & Tomelleri, S. (2009). The transmission of racial attitudes within the family. *Developmental Psychology, 45,* 586–591.

Catlett, C., Ostrosky, M.M., & Santos, R.M. (2012). *Discovering and exploring DEC's research and practical resources.* Paper presented at the NAEYC Professional Development Conference, Indianapolis, IN.

CAST. (2011). *Universal Design for Learning Guidelines version 2.0.* Wakefield, MA: Author.

Center for Public Education. (2012). *The United States of education: The changing demographics of the United States and their schools.* Retrieved December 12, 2014, from http://www.centerforpublic education.org/You-May-Also-Be-Interested-In-landing-page-level/Organizing-a-School -YMABI/The-United-States-of-education-The-changing-demographics-of-the-United-States-and -their-schools.html

Children Now. (2004). *Fall colors: Prime time diversity report 2003–04.* Oakland, CA: Children Now.

Christian, L.G. (2006). Understanding families: Applying family systems theory to early childhood practice. *Young Exceptional Children, 61*(1), 12–20.

Civil Rights Act of 1964, Title 42, U.S.C. §§ 2000 *et seq.*

Clark, C. (1969). Television and social control: Some observations on the portrayal of ethnic minorities. *Television Quarterly, 9*(2), 18–32.

Clark, C. (1972). Race, identification, and television violence. In G.A. Comstock, E.A. Rubinstein, & J.P. Murray (Eds.), *Television and social behavior,* Vol. 5: *Television's effects: Further explorations* (pp. 120–184). Washington, DC: U.S. Government Printing Office.

Cook, C., Williams, K., Guerra, N., Kim, T., & Sadek, S. (2010). Predictors of bullying and victimization in childhood and adolescence: A meta-analytic investigation. *School Psychology Quarterly, 25*(2), 65–83.

Council for Exceptional Children–Division for Early Childhood & National Association for the Education of Young Children (DEC/NAEYC). (2009). *Early childhood inclusion: A summary.* Chapel Hill, NC: University of North Carolina, FPG Child Development Institute.

Cox-Petersen, A. (2011). The makeup of families today: Culturally relevant strategies to enhance partnerships. In A. Cox-Petersen (Ed.), *Educational partnerships: Connecting schools, families, and the community* (pp. 79–106). Fullerton, CA: Sage.

Davis, S., Howell, P., & Cook, F. (2002). Sociodynamic relationships between children who stutter and their non-stuttering classmates. *Journal of Child Psychology and Psychiatry, 43*(7), 939–947.

Derman-Sparks, L., & ABC Task Force. (1989). *Anti-bias curriculum: Tools for empowering young children.* Washington, DC: National Association for the Education of Young Children.

Derman-Sparks, L., Tanaka Higa, C., & Sparks, B. (1980). Children, race, and racism: How race awareness develops. *Bulletin, 11*(3–4), 3–9. Retrieved December 1, 2014, from http://www.teachingfor change.org/wp-content/uploads/2012/08/ec_childrenraceracism_english.pdf

Diamond, K., & Innes, F. (2001). The origins of young children's attitudes toward peers with disabilities. In M.J. Guralnick (Ed.), *Early childhood inclusion: Focus on change* (pp. 159–177). Baltimore, MD: Paul H. Brookes Publishing Co.

Dickinson, D.K. (2001). Book reading in preschool classrooms: Is recommended practice common? In D.K. Dickinson & P.O. Tabors (Eds.), *Beginning literacy with language: Young children learning at home and school* (pp. 175–203). Baltimore, MD: Paul H. Brookes Publishing Co.

Diller, J.V., & Moule, J. (2005). *Cultural competence: A primer for educators.* Belmont, CA: Thomson Wadsworth.

Dixon, T., & Linz, D. (2000). Race and the misrepresentation of victimization on local television. *Communication Research, 27*(5), 547–573.

Dyson, L. (2005). Kindergarten children's understanding and attitudes toward people with disabilities. *Topics in Early Childhood Special Education, 25*(2), 95–105.

Eagly, A.H., & Chaiken, S. (1993). *The psychology of attitudes.* Fort Worth, TX: Harcourt.

Education for All Handicapped Children Act of 1977, Title 20, U.S.C. §§ 1400 *et seq.*

Engel, D.M. (1991). Law, culture, and children with disabilities: Educational rights and construction of difference. *Duke Law Journal, 1,* 166–205.

Favazza, P.C. (1998). Preparing for children with disabilities in early childhood classrooms. *Early Childhood Education Journal, 25*(4), 255–258.

Mouzourou, C., Favazza, P.C. Ostrosky, M.M., Leboeuf, L. (2015). Universal design for learning (UDL) in inclusive early childhood classes. Manuscript in progress.

Favazza, P.C., LaRoe, J., & Odom, S.L. (Eds.). (1999). *Special Friends: A manual for creating accepting environments.* Boulder, CO: Roots and Wings.

Favazza, P.C., LaRoe, J., Phillipsen, L., & Kumar, P. (2000). Representing young children with disabilities in classroom environments. *Young Exceptional Children, 3*(3), 2–8.

Favazza, P.C., & Odom, S.L. (1996). Use of the Acceptance Scale with kindergarten-age children. *Journal of Early Intervention, 2*(3), 232–248.

Favazza, P.C., & Odom, S.L. (1997). Promoting positive attitudes of kindergarten-age children toward individuals with disabilities. *Exceptional Children, 63*(3), 405–418.

Favazza, P.C., & Odom, S.L. (1999). Individuals with disabilities representation scale. In P.C. Favazza, J. LaRoe, & S.L. Odom (Eds.), *Special Friends: A manual for creating accepting environments* (pp. 62–64). Boulder, CO: Roots and Wings.

Favazza, P.C., Phillipsen, L., & Kumar, P. (2000). Strategies designed to promote and measure acceptance: A follow-up study of efficacy and reliability. *Exceptional Children, 66*(4), 491–508.

Fawcett, C.A., & Markson, L. (2010). Similarity predicts liking in 3-year-old children. *Journal of Experimental Child Psychology, 105*(4), 345–358.

Fitzgerald, D. (1999). Children of lesbian and gay parents: A review of literature. *Marriage and Family Review, 29*(1), 57–75.

Fox, L., & Lentini, R.H. (2006). "You got it!" Teaching social and emotional skills. *Young Children, 61*(6), 36–42.

Fuchs, D., & Fuchs, L.S. (1994). Inclusive schools movement and the radicalization of special education reform. *Exceptional Children, 60*(4), 294–309.

Garman, M.A. (2005). Six key factors for changing preservice teachers' attitudes/beliefs about diversity. *Educational Studies: A Journal of the American Educational Studies Association, 38*(3), 275–286. doi:10.1207/s15326993es3803_7

Gerber, P.J. (1977, June). Awareness of handicapping conditions and sociometric status in an integrated pre-school setting. *Mental Retardation, 15*(3), 24–25.

Hamlin, J.K., Mahajan, N., Liberman, Z., & Wynn, K. (2013). Not like me = bad: Infants prefer those who harm dissimilar others. *Psychological Sciences, 24*(4), 589–594. doi:10.1177/0956797612457785

Horne, M. (1985). *Attitudes toward handicapped students: Professional, peer and parent reactions.* Hillsdale, NJ: Lawrence Erlbaum Associates.

Horning, K.T., Lindgren, M.V., & Schliesman, M. (2013). *A few observations on publishing in 2012.* The Cooperative Children's Book Center, University of Wisconsin–Madison. Retrieved December 1, 2014, from http://ccbc.education.wisc.edu/books/choiceintro13.asp

Hughes, D., Rodriguez, J., Smith, E., Johnson, D., Stevenson, H., & Spicer, P. (2006). Parents' ethnic-racial socialization practices: A review of research and directions for future study. *Developmental Psychology, 42,* 747–770.

Hunt, P. (1991). Discrimination: Disabled people and the media. *Contact, 70,* 45–48.

Hunter, L., & Elias, M.J. (1999). Interracial friendships, multicultural sensitivity, and social competence: How are they related? *Journal of Applied Developmental Psychology, 20,* 551–573.

Innes, F.K., & Diamond, K.E. (1999). Typically developing children's interactions with peers with disabilities: Relationships between mothers' comments and children's ideas about disabilities. *Topics in Early Childhood Special Education, 19,* 103–111.

Jeynes, W.H. (2005). A meta-analysis of the relation of parental involvement to urban elementary school student academic achievement. *Urban Education, 40,* 237–269.

Johnson, D.W., & Johnson, F.P. (1991). *Joining together, group theory and group skills* (4th ed.). Upper Saddle River, NJ: Prentice Hall.

Johnson, D., & Lewis, C. (1998). Introduction: Children's and young adult literature. *African American Review, 32*(1), 5–7.

Johnson, R.T., & Johnson, D.W. (1994). An overview of cooperative learning. In J.S. Thousand, R.A. Villa, & A.I. Nevin (Eds.), *Creativity and collaborative learning: A practical guide to empowering students and teachers* (pp. 31–44). Baltimore, MD: Paul H. Brookes Publishing Co.

Jones, R.L. (1984). *Attitude and attitude change in special education: Theory and practice.* Reston, VA: Council of Exceptional Children.

Jones, R.L., & Sisk, D. (1970). Early perceptions of orthopedic disability: A developmental study. *Rehabilitation Literature, 31,* 34–38.

Jordan, P., & Hernandez-Reif, M. (2009). Reexamination of young children's racial attitudes and skin tone preferences. *Journal of Black Psychology, 35*(3), 388–403.

Joshua, M. (2002). Inside picture books: Where are children of color? *Educational Horizons, 80*(3), 125–132.

Kissen, R.M. (2002). *Getting ready for Benjamin: Preparing teachers for sexual diversity in the classroom.* Lanham, MD: Rowman and Littlefield.

Lamme, L.L., & Lamme, L.A. (2002). Welcoming children from gay families into our schools. *Education Leadership, 59*(4), 65–69.

Lieber, J., Capell, K., Sandall, S.R., Wolfberg, P., Horn, E., & Beckman, P. (1998). Inclusive preschool programs: Teachers' beliefs and practices. *Early Childhood Research Quarterly, 13,* 87–105.

Manhajan, N., & Wynn, K. (2012). Origins of "us" versus "them": Prelinguistic infants prefer similar others. *Cognition, 124*(2), 227–233.

Mastro, D., Behm-Morawitz, E., & Kopacz, M. (2008). Exposure to television portrayals of Latinos: The implications of aversive racism and social identity theory. *Human Communication Research, 34,* 1–27.

Meadan, H., Ostrosky, M.M., Santos, R.M., & Snodgrass, M. (2013). How can I help? Prompting procedures to support children's learning. *Young Exceptional Children, 16*(4), 31–39.

Mohay, H., & Reid, E. (2006). The inclusion of children with disability in childcare: The influence of experience, training and attitudes of childcare staff. *Australian Journal of Early Childhood, 31*(1), 1–9.

Munyi, C.W. (2012). Past and present perceptions towards disability: A historical perspective. *Disability Studies Quarterly, 32*(2). Retrieved November 2014, from http://dsq-sds.org/article/view/3197/3068

Nasatir, D., & Horn, E. (2003). Addressing disability as a part of diversity through classroom children's literature. *Young Exceptional Children, 6*(4), 2–10. doi:10.1177/109625060300600401

National Association for the Education of Young Children (NAEYC). (1995). *Position statement: Responding to linguistic and cultural diversity recommendations for effective early childhood education.* Retrieved December 1, 2014, from http://www.naeyc.org/files/naeyc/file/positions/PSDIV98.PDF

National Association for the Education of Young Children (NAEYC). (2009). *Position statement: Developmentally appropriate practice in early childhood programs serving children from birth through age 8.* Retrieved December 1, 2014, from http://www.naeyc.org/files/naeyc/file/positions/position%20statement%20Web.pdf

National Center for Education Statistics. (2014). *The condition of education: Children and youth with disabilities.* Retrieved December 2, 2014, from http://nces.ed.gov/programs/coe/indicator_cgg.asp

National Education Association. (n.d.-a). *Diversity toolkit: Cultural competence for educators.* Retrieved December 2, 2014, from http://www.nea.org/tools/30402.htm

National Education Association. (n.d.-b). *Diversity toolkit introduction.* Retrieved December 2, 2014, from http://www.nea.org/tools/diversity-toolkit-introduction.html

Nemeth, K. (2012). State policies on dual language learners in early childhood. *Colorin Colorado.* Retrieved May 12, 2015, from http://www.colorincolorado.org/article/50574

Nowicki, E.A., & Sandieson, R. (2002). A meta-analysis of school-age children's attitudes towards persons with physical or intellectual disabilities. *International Journal of Disability, Development, and Education, 49,* 243–265.

Odom, S.L., & Bailey, D. (2001). Inclusive preschool programs: Classroom ecology and child outcomes. In M.J. Guralnick (Ed.), *Early childhood inclusion: Focus on change* (pp. 253–276). Baltimore, MD: Paul H. Brookes Publishing Co.

Odom, S.L., & Brown, W.H. (1993). Social interaction skills for young children with disabilities in integrated settings. In C.A. Peck, S.L. Odom, & D.D. Bricker (Eds.), *Integrating young children with disabilities into community settings* (pp. 39–64). Baltimore, MD: Paul H. Brookes Publishing Co.

Ostrosky, M.M., & Favazza, P. (2008). *Establishing the efficacy of the Special Friends program* (PR/Award No. R324A080071). Washington, DC: Institute of Education Sciences.

Ostrosky, M.M., Mouzourou, C., Favazza, P.C., & Leboeuf, L. (2012, October). *Evaluating the acceptance of children with disabilities: The Special Friends program.* Paper presented at DEC's 28th Annual International Conference on Young Children with Special Needs and Their Families, Minneapolis, MN.

Park, H., & Ostrosky, M.M. (2013). What typically developing children's parents say when they read books about disabilities. *Topics in Early Childhood Special Education, 33*(4), 225–236. doi:10.1177/0271121413497104

Peretti, P.O., & Sydney, T.M. (1984). Parental toy choice stereotyping and its effects on child toy preference and sex-role typing. *Social Behavior and Personality, 12,* 213–216.

Pescosolido, B., Grauerholz, E., & Milkie, M. (1997). Culture and conflict: The portrayal of blacks in U.S. children's picture books through the mid and late twentieth century. *American Sociological Review, 3,* 443–464.

Pettigrew, T.F., & Tropp, L.R. (2000). Does intergroup contact reduce prejudice? Recent meta-analytic findings. In S. Oskamp (Ed.), *Reducing prejudice and discrimination: The Claremont Symposium on applied social psychology* (pp. 93–114). Mahwah, NJ: Lawrence Erlbaum Associates.

Powell-Hopson, D., & Hopson, D. (1992). Implications of doll color preferences among black preschool children and white preschool children. In A. Burlew, K. Hoard, W. Banks, H. McAdoo, & D. Azibo (Eds.), *African American psychology: Theory, research, and practice* (pp. 183–189). Newbury Park, CA: Sage.

Rehabilitation Act of 1973, Title 29, U.S.C. §§ 701 *et seq.*

Rivadeneyra, R., Ward, M., & Gordon, M. (2007). Distorted reflections: Media exposure and Latino adolescents' conceptions of self. *Media Psychology, 9,* 261–290.

Roethler, J. (1998). Reading in color: Children's book illustrations and identity formation for black children in the United States. *African American Review, 32,* 95–105.

Sailor, W., Gee, K., & Karasoff, P. (1993). Full inclusion and school restructuring. In M.E. Snell (Ed.), *Instruction of students with severe disabilities* (pp. 1–30). Upper Saddle River, NJ: Prentice Hall.

Sainato, D.M., & Carta, J.J. (1992). Classroom influences on the development of social competence in young children with disabilities. In S.L. Odom, S.R. McConnell, & M.A. McEvoy (Eds.), *Social competence of young children with disabilities: Issues and strategies for intervention* (pp. 93–109). Baltimore, MD: Paul H. Brookes Publishing Co.

Santos, R.M., Cheatham, G.A., & Duran, L. (Eds.). (2012). *Supporting young children who are dual language learners with or at-risk for disabilities* (Young Exceptional Children Monograph Series No. 14). Missoula, MT: Division for Early Childhood of the Council for Exceptional Children.

Sinclair, S., Dunn, E., & Lowery, B.S. (2005). The relationship between parental racial attitudes and children's implicit prejudices. *Journal of Experimental Social Psychology, 41,* 283–289.

Siraj-Blatchford, I., & Clarke, P. (2000). *Supporting identity, diversity and language in the early years.* Philadelphia, PA: Open University Press.

Stockall, N., Dennis, L., & Miller, M. (2012). Right from the start: Universal design for preschool. *Teaching Exceptional Children, 45*(1), 10–17.

Stoneman, Z., Cantrell, M.L., & Hoover-Dempsey, K. (1983). The association between play materials and social behavior in a mainstreamed preschool: A naturalistic investigation. *Journal of Applied Developmental Psychology, 4,* 163–174.

Taylor, A. (2000). *The roots of racism.* Retrieved December 12, 2014, from http://socialistworker.org/2002-2/431/431_08_Racism.shtml

Thornton, A., & Camburn, D. (1987). The influence of the family on premarital sexual attitudes and behavior. *Demography, 24,* 323–340.

Trawick-Smith, J. (1992). The physical classroom environment: How it affects young children's play and development. *Dimensions of Early Childhood, 20*(2), 19–30.

Triandis, H.C. (1971). *Attitude and attitude change.* New York, NY: John Wiley & Sons.

Triandis, H.C., Adamopoulos, J., & Brinberg, D. (1984). Perspectives and issues in the study of attitudes. In R. Jones (Ed.), *Attitudes and attitude change in special education: Theory and practice* (pp. 21–41). Reston, VA: Council for Exceptional Children.

United Nations Convention on the Rights of Persons with Disabilities. (2006). Retrieved on May 12, 2015, from http://www.refworld.org/docid/4680cd212.html

United Nations Convention on the Rights of the Child. (1990). Retrieved on May 6, 2015, from http://www.ohchr.org/en/professionalinterest/pages/crc.aspx

US Education Amendments of 1972, Title 20, U.S.C. §§ 1681 *et seq.*

Vittrup, B., & Holden, G.W. (2010). Exploring the impact of educational television and parent–child discussions on children's racial attitudes. *Analyses of Social Issues and Public Policy, 10*(1), 192–214.

Waldron, N.L., & McLeskey, J. (1998). The effects of an inclusive school program on students with mild and severe learning disabilities. *Exceptional Children, 64*(3), 395–405.

Weinraub, M., Clemens, L.P., Sockloff, A., Ethridge, T., Gracely, E., & Myers, B. (1984). The development of sex role stereotypes in the third year: Relationships to gender labeling, gender identity, sex-typed toy preference, and family characteristics. *Child Development, 55,* 1493–1503.

Williams, H.A. (2005). *Self-taught: American education in slavery and freedom.* Chapel Hill, NC: University of North Carolina Press.

Wood, J., & Fabrigar, L. (2012). Attitudes. *Oxford Bibliographies Online: Psychology.* doi:10.1093/obo/9780199828340-0074

Yu, S.Y., & Ostrosky, M.M. (2012). Young children's understanding of disabilities: Implications for attitude development and inclusive education. In B. Spodek & O. Saracho (Eds.), *Handbook of research on the education of young children* (pp. 345–354). New York, NY: Routledge.

Yu, S.Y., Ostrosky, M.M., & Fowler, S.A. (2012). Measuring young children's attitudes toward peers with disabilities: Highlights from the research. *Topics in Early Childhood Special Education, 32*(3), 132–142. doi:10.1177/0271121412453175

Yu, S.Y., Ostrosky, M., & Fowler, S. (2014). Children's friendship development: A comparative study. *Early Childhood Research and Practice, 13*(1). Retrieved January 4, 2015, from http://ecrp.uiuc.edu/v13n1/yu.html

Index

Tables and figures are indicated by *t* and *f*, respectively.